soul

soul

recipes from judith tabron & friends

at soul bar & bistro

RANDOM HOUSE
NEW ZEALAND

Though my name appears on the front cover, this book is a team effort. I would like to thank Peter Thornley and the kitchen team for recipe testing and the production of the food for photography. I would also like to thank Geeling for being the best side-kick ever.

judith tabron

A catalogue record for this book is available from the National Library of New Zealand

A RANDOM HOUSE BOOK
published by
Random House New Zealand
18 Poland Road, Glenfield, Auckland, New Zealand

www.randomhouse.co.nz

First published 2005

text © 2005 Judith Tabron and individual chefs as credited
photographs © 2005 Stephen Robinson except photos on pages 6, 9 and front cover right and back cover top
left which are © Wayne Wilson, photo page 98 courtesy of Bill Marchetti

The moral rights of the author have been asserted

ISBN 1 86941 754 2

Cover photograph: (left) Stephen Robinson; (right) Wayne Wilson
Cover design: nick turzynski, redinc., Auckland
Design: nick turzynski, redinc., Auckland
Printed in China

cOntents

introduction

Well, here it is at last! After many years of being prodded by friends and industry colleagues, I have finally put together a cookbook. It is based on recipes used at Soul Bar & Bistro, in Auckland's Viaduct Harbour, since its opening four years ago. It also features recipes from guest chefs who have been involved with the evolution of Soul's cuisine during that period, most of whom have designed menus specifically for the restaurant and have featured at events held there.

When I joined forces with well-known entrepreneur Eric Watson in 2001 to establish Soul, I was keen to bring to Viaduct Harbour and to Auckland a busy, exciting and vibrant place for casual business and occasion dining, at all times of the day and night. It is, therefore, a true bistro. It was my wish in particular that as many people as possible should have the opportunity of enjoying Soul's wonderful location and outlook.

The collection of recipes in this book is a small sample of the offerings prepared at Soul. All of them have been on Soul's menu over the years, in fact many of them are particular favourites of mine which I have used from time to time over many years in the restaurant and hospitality industry. It has been an interesting exercise to reduce recipes to cater for six people when they were designed to produce 20 to 30 servings. The chefs at Soul have worked particularly hard to scale the quantities to enable these recipes to be prepared at home.

In addition to Soul's recipe selection, this book includes three recipes each from Charlie Trotter, Bill Marchetti, Greg Malouf, Philip Johnson, Stephanie Alexander and our very own Geeling. I am delighted these chefs were prepared to permit me to publish their recipes and bring a further taste dimension to your cooking and eating pleasure.

During my years in the hospitality industry, I have realised the benefit of capturing international influences to develop our menus. There is a continual requirement to stay 'up with the play'. I like to travel and be exposed to food and restaurant styles and environments throughout the world. I am always looking for the next 'sexy' trend to bring back to New Zealand to tickle the fancy of my clientele; to lead, rather than follow, the local market.

In certain circumstances it is difficult to import a new cuisine style without importing the food production skills at the same time. That is why I have, for many years, followed a policy of bringing international guest chefs to New Zealand. The presence of these international chefs at Soul not only pleases the customers but also enables our kitchen staff to learn new skills. The knowledge and passion of these guests assists the development of our keen New Zealand chefs, and helps with the retention of the talent pool here. There is no question that the introduction of new styles, ingredients and methods by my guest chefs has added much to the tapestry of Soul's development.

Over the years, New Zealand food producers have widened their product ranges. I would like to think this is partly because of the demands of the international chefs. Often these chefs have tried to bring their own products into the country — and have promptly had them confiscated by New Zealand Customs. In many cases we have been able to substitute New Zealand ingredients and products and, sometimes, the chefs have commented that they have achieved a better result. This can only be good for New Zealand, as the chefs then seek to have our products introduced to their countries of origin.

Sourcing the ingredients for a guest chef's recipes has always been a challenge. In 1993, Bill Marchetti was looking for a particular potato for his gnocchi (the recipe is on page 137 and the dish is still on Soul's menu). We visited the markets and proceeded to cut potatoes in half until we found the required variety, with a yellow centre. That variety, Agria, has now become very popular in New Zealand. Another time Bill requested sheep's ricotta and yoghurt. You would have thought that these products would have been readily available in a country with so many sheep! However, in the end, it was necessary to use the services of Massey University (Agri Dairy Research) to make them for us.

Greg Malouf required pigeons. All we could get were 'rejects' from a carrier-pigeon breeder. For Greg, these measured up, and he said they

were 'fantastic quality'. He also wanted milk-fed lamb which, surprisingly, was not and is still not available in New Zealand. To prepare his modern Middle Eastern recipes, we needed to source imported products such as sumac, vine leaves, orange-blossom water and fairy floss which were not previously available. You will now find them in most gourmet food stores.

We have still some way to go. Although our overall quality is high there are still a number of gaps in availability of certain product types, distribution and packaging. As Stephanie Alexander quite rightly pointed out, it is a strange situation when our beautiful Bluff oysters are delivered only in plastic pottles rather than shucked to order in restaurants. Both the seafood industry and restaurateurs still have plenty to do, and I believe we will continue to meet the challenge.

judith tabron

soul bar & bistro

meat & poultry

roast rack of lamb

with fennel, fresh mint and toasted almond salad

At Soul, we serve this with the crispy potato and goat's cheese terrine (recipe on page 52).

4 medium-size fennel bulbs
juice of 1 lemon

muscatel dressing

4 teaspoons almond oil
2 teaspoons grapeseed oil
1 teaspoon clear thyme honey
2 teaspoons muscatel vinegar
salt and freshly milled black pepper

3 teaspoons peanut oil
½ cup slivered almonds
12 mint leaves

lamb

3 tablespoons extra virgin olive oil
6 racks of new-season lamb, each approximately 325g
salt and freshly milled black pepper
1 teaspoon sumac
1 teaspoon fresh thyme, finely chopped

Serves 6

Preheat the oven to 220°C.

Remove the outer layer of the fennel and discard. Slice bulb to a thickness of 1mm. Place in ice water with the lemon juice.

To make the dressing, whisk together the oils, honey and vinegar. Season to taste.

Heat the peanut oil in a frypan over a medium heat and fry the almonds for 3 to 4 minutes until golden. Drain on absorbent paper.

Drain the fennel and toss with almonds, mint and dressing. Season to taste.

To prepare the lamb, heat olive oil in a frypan over a medium to high heat. Season lamb with salt and pepper and rub with sumac and chopped thyme.

Cook each rack on one side for about 3 minutes then place them all in the oven for a further 4 minutes.

Remove lamb from oven and rest for 6 to 8 minutes.

To serve, place a pile of salad in the middle of each plate. Divide the lamb into cutlets and arrange neatly in front of the salad. Splash over the remaining dressing.

cabernet-braised beef short ribs
with parsnip mash and autumn herb salad

red wine marinade

3 tablespoons canola oil

½ cup diced carrot

½ cup diced onion

½ cup diced leek (white part only)

3 cloves garlic, peeled and crushed

750ml bottle red wine

1 bay leaf

4 sprigs thyme

2 sprigs parsley

6 black peppercorns

25g root ginger

2 juniper berries

¼ cinnamon quill

1 star anise

6 pieces Hereford prime beef short ribs, 6cm wide, each about 400g

cabernet vinaigrette

2 tablespoons extra virgin olive oil

4 tablespoons grapeseed or canola oil

1 tablespoon peanut oil

1 tablespoon cabernet sauvignon vinegar

sea salt and freshly milled black pepper

¼ cup peanut oil

sea salt and freshly milled black pepper

flour for dusting

4 sprigs thyme

2 bay leaves

1 medium-size onion, peeled and cut into 1cm cubes

1 large carrot, cut into 1cm cubes

1 stick celery, cut into 1cm cubes

10 cloves garlic, peeled

6 cups veal stock (recipe page 140)

2 cups golden chicken stock (recipe page 139)

1 parsnip mash recipe (recipe page 73)

salt and freshly milled black and white pepper

herb salad

¼ cup tarragon

½ cup chervil

¼ cup flat-leaf parsley

¼ cup baby chard leaves

¼ cup snipped 3cm long chives

Serves 6

To make the marinade, heat the oil in a large saucepan. Add the prepared vegetables and garlic and sauté for 2 to 3 minutes. Add the red wine and remaining marinade ingredients and simmer until all alcohol has evaporated (approximately 4 to 5 minutes). Allow to cool.

Marinate beef short ribs for 12 to 24 hours but no longer.

To make the vinaigrette, whisk together the oils and vinegar. Season to taste and set aside.

When ready to prepare the ribs, preheat the oven to 180°C. Remove ribs from marinade and pat dry. Pass the remaining marinade through a sieve and discard the debris.

Place the marinade in a saucepan and bring to a simmer. Skim off any impurities that come to the surface. Reduce by half and set aside.

Heat the peanut oil in a large frypan until very hot. Season the meat and dust with flour. Shake off excess flour and cook ribs for 3 to 4 minutes on each side until well coloured.

Remove the meat from the frypan and place in a heavy, ovenproof casserole dish. Scatter thyme sprigs and bay leaves over the ribs.

Discard excess oil from the pan and sauté the vegetables and garlic until lightly coloured. Add the reduced marinade and veal stock and chicken stock and bring to a simmer. Pour over the short ribs until they are covered with stock. Cover the casserole dish with a lid and braise in the oven for 4 to 5 hours until tender.

When the meat is cooked, remove it from the casserole and set aside to keep warm. Strain the liquid through a muslin-lined chinois or fine strainer into a heavy-based saucepan, and discard the debris. Bring back to the boil and simmer to reduce the braising liquid to sauce consistency (approximately 2½ cups).

To assemble, place a spoonful of parsnip mash to the side of each plate. Rest the ribs in the middle of the plate and season.

To make the salad, pick the leaves from the stems of the tarragon, chervil and parsley. Place in a bowl then toss with the chard and chopped chives. Toss lightly with the cabernet vinaigrette.

Pour a little marinade sauce over and around the meat, and place a neat pile of salad on each rib.

grilled farmed venison chops with caramelised peppers and pomegranate

The delicious basil oil used in this recipe will keep for a day in the refrigerator or frozen for months, with little loss of colour and flavour.

12 red peppers (capsicums)

basil oil

2 cups basil leaves, loosely packed

½ cup grapeseed oil

12 venison chops, each approximately 90–100g

1 teaspoon finely chopped thyme

sea salt and freshly milled black pepper

4 tablespoons grapeseed oil

3 tablespoons pomegranate molasses

42 cloves garlic, roasted in olive oil, in 160°C oven for 35 minutes

fresh basil leaves to garnish

Serves 6

Prick the peppers all over and place on a heated grill or barbecue. Turn them over the heat until the skin is completely blistered. Place in a large bowl and cover tightly with cling film. Leave to sweat for 30 minutes, then peel off the skins, detach the stalks, cut each pepper in half and remove the seeds. Drain on absorbent paper.

To prepare the oil, blanch the basil for 15 seconds in boiling, salted water. Refresh immediately in ice water, drain and squeeze dry.

Place half the oil and half the basil into a blender and purée. Add the remaining oil and basil and purée again.

Pour the purée into a muslin cloth or jelly bag set over a bowl, and allow to filter for about 1 hour.

Once filtered, discard the muslin cloth and the remaining purée. Set oil aside until required.

To prepare the chops, season with thyme, salt and pepper. Heat half of the grapeseed oil in a large, heavy sauté pan over a high heat. Add the chops and cook for 2 to 3 minutes until brown. Turn the chops and cook for a further 3 minutes, until medium rare. Tilt the pan to one side and baste the chops with the oil that is in the pan. Remove chops from pan and rest for 3 to 4 minutes.

Clean the pan and heat remaining oil over a medium to high heat. Add the peppers and sauté for 3 minutes. Add the pomegranate molasses and cook for a further 3 minutes until the peppers are caramelised. Toss in the roasted garlic cloves, keeping the pan moving to prevent the peppers from catching. Adjust seasonings to taste.

To serve, place a neat pile of caramelised peppers at the side of each plate. Arrange two chops to rest against the peppers and then scatter seven garlic cloves on and around the meat. Drizzle with the basil oil and garnish with fresh basil leaves.

meatloaf on red kumara and balsamic mash with tamarind chutney

This is a great winter dish. The tamarind chutney recipe comes from our Fijian-Indian chef Sunita Devi. Sunita was a foundation employee at Ramses in 1989, and still works with us at Soul today. Tamarind pulp can be purchased from Asian or Indian Emporiums. The meatloaf is best prepared a day in advance.

tamarind chutney

200g tamarind pulp (the darker the pulp the better)

3 cups water

60ml olive oil

50g onion flakes

2 cloves garlic, peeled and crushed

20g root ginger, peeled and crushed

½ curry leaf

1 teaspoon black mustard seeds

1 teaspoon cumin seeds

1 teaspoon chilli powder

20g dessicated coconut

250g sugar

sea salt and freshly milled black pepper

meatloaf

2 tablespoons olive oil

50g diced onion

1 large clove garlic, peeled and finely chopped

225g shiitake mushrooms, chopped

115g white mushrooms, chopped

115g eggplant, diced

½ cup cream

1½ teaspoons salt

freshly milled black pepper

900g in total minced lamb, veal and pork

1 teaspoon chopped fresh thyme leaves

1 teaspoon ground cumin

2 whole eggs, lightly beaten

350g streaky bacon slices

red kumara and balsamic mash

1.5kg red kumara

1½ tablespoons unsalted butter

¼ teaspoon ground cinnamon

⅓ teaspoon freshly grated or ground nutmeg

¾ cup milk

1 teaspoon salt

freshly milled black pepper

1 tablespoon balsamic vinegar

Serves 6

Preheat oven to 200°C.

Heat the oil in a large pan. Add onion and garlic and sauté until light golden-brown. Add mushrooms, eggplant and cream, salt and pepper and simmer for 3 to 4 minutes. Remove from heat and cool to room temperature.

In a large bowl, combine mince with cooled creamed vegetables. Add thyme, cumin and eggs.

Heat a little oil in a pan and gently sauté 1 teaspoon of the mixture. Taste to check seasoning and adjust if necessary.

Lightly grease a loaf tin and line with the bacon, leaving enough bacon hanging over the edges to fold over and cover the top. Lightly pack meatloaf mixture into the tin to 1.5cm above the rim. Fold bacon over the top and cover with foil.

Place loaf tin in a roasting tray and fill the tray with boiling water to halfway up the sides of the tin. Bake for 30 minutes, then remove foil and bake for 1 hour further. Remove meatloaf from oven and allow to cool completely. Place in fridge until required.

To make the chutney, soak the tamarind pulp in the cold water for 1 hour. Remove the seeds and stringy bits, but retain the liquid.

In a large, heavy-based saucepan, heat the oil, add the onion, garlic, ginger, curry leaf, mustard and cumin seeds and cook on a low heat until golden brown. Add the chilli powder, coconut and tamarind pulp, with all its liquid. Add the sugar and season. Cook on a low heat for 1 hour, stirring all the time (this sauce burns very easily, so be careful). Taste, and add a little extra sugar if the chutney is sour. Cook for a further 30 minutes until thick.

To make the mash, bake the kumara whole in their skins in a hot oven until cooked (approximately 1 hour). Use a skewer to check they are soft all the way through. When cool enough to handle, peel and mash, or put flesh through a mincer or mouli. Keep warm.

Melt the butter in a saucepan until it browns. Stir in the cinnamon and nutmeg. Remove from heat, stir in the milk, then return to the stove and bring the milk to the boil. Add the kumara mash and combine. Season, then stir in balsamic vinegar.

To serve, heat 2 tablespoons of olive oil in a large frypan or electric frypan. Slice the chilled meatloaf into six even portions and fry on both sides until browned. Reduce heat, cover and cook until heated all the way through. (This can also be done in the oven.)

Arrange the mash in the centre of each plate. Place a slice of meatloaf on top and finish with a good tablespoon of tamarind chutney.

grilled cOrn-fed chicken and caramelised parsnips with rosemary and honey vinaigrette

This is my favourite dish after a late night — I always order it for lunch.

caramelised parsnips

4 medium-size parsnips

2 tablespoons unsalted butter

2 sprigs thyme

1 teaspoon salt

2 tablespoons peanut oil

2 tablespoons honey

2 tablespoons unsalted butter

sea salt and freshly milled black pepper

chicken

6 corn-fed chicken breasts, each approximately 220g

sea salt and freshly milled black pepper

butter for rubbing

4 tablespoons extra virgin olive oil

3 tablespoons unsalted butter

36 cloves garlic, roasted in olive oil in 160°C oven for 35 minutes

6 sprigs thyme

rosemary and honey vinaigrette

3 tablespoons grapeseed oil

3 tablespoons extra virgin olive oil

1 tablespoon honey

1 teaspoon low-salt soya sauce

1 teaspoon chopped rosemary leaves

sea salt and freshly milled white pepper

Serves 6

Peel parsnips, cut into quarters lengthwise and remove the core. Cut each quarter into fingers.

Place parsnips in a saucepan, cover with water and bring to the boil. Add the butter, thyme and salt. Cover with a lid and cook until tender (approximately 10 minutes). Remove from heat and drain in a colander.

Preheat oven to 200°C. Gently ease back the skin of the chicken breasts and season underneath. Rub each breast with a little butter.

Heat the oil in a large frypan over medium to high heat. Add the chicken, skin-side down, and sauté for 3 minutes to lightly colour. Turn the chicken and cook for another 3 minutes.

Add the butter, garlic cloves and thyme. Transfer to the hot oven and bake for 6 to 8 minutes, basting the chicken with the butter as it melts.

While the chicken is cooking, heat the peanut oil in a large sauté pan over a medium to high heat. Add the cooled parsnips and cook to a light golden-brown (approximately 5 to 7 minutes). Add the honey and remaining 2 tablespoons butter. Allow to caramelise, then season to taste.

To prepare the dressing, whisk together the oils, honey and soya sauce. Stir in the chopped rosemary. Season to taste.

To serve, place a portion of the caramelised parsnips in the middle of each plate. Rest a chicken breast on top of the parsnips and scatter the garlic cloves around. Drizzle the dressing over and around the chicken.

soul bar & bistro

fish

cedar-planked salmon
with grilled polenta and apple cider butter sauce

The Beekman Arms in Rhinebeck, New York is where this dish comes from. It is not far from the Culinary Institute of America where I spent some time attending courses on nutrition and Mediterranean food. The Native Americans cooked their salmon in this way. I buy untreated cedar shingles from Rosenfield and Kidson, a timber supplier in Auckland. They do look at me strangely when I ask them to chop the wood into small planks. Any untreated fruit wood can also be used, such as apple or cherry, and the planks can be reused if they aren't too burnt. Other types of fish can also be smoked this way.

apple cider butter sauce

330ml apple cider

2 shallots, peeled and chopped

1 Granny Smith apple, peeled, cored and diced

300g unsalted butter, cubed

sea salt and freshly milled white pepper

polenta

2 tablespoons olive oil

1 portion polenta (recipe page 137)

flour for dusting

6 salmon fillets, each approximately 200g, pin bones removed

2 tablespoons melted butter

2 teaspoons mustard powder

sea salt and freshly milled black pepper

6 handfuls rocket leaves

1 lemon, cut into six wedges

Serves 6

To make the sauce, place the cider, shallots and apple in a heavy-based saucepan. Over a medium-high heat, reduce the liquid to a syrupy consistency.

Pass through a fine strainer and discard the pulp. Return the syrup to the saucepan and whisk in the butter over a low heat. Don't boil the sauce when adding the butter or it will split. The harder you whisk, the thicker the sauce will become. The sauce is at the right consistency when it coats the back of a spoon. Season to taste.

To prevent the butter from setting, keep the sauce in a warm place or place the container holding the sauce into a shallow bath of warm water.

Turn the oven grill to high. While it is heating, prepare the polenta. Heat the oil in a non-stick frypan. While the oil is heating, lightly dust the polenta with flour then place gently in pan. Lightly brown each side.

While browning the polenta, dampen the cedar planks (two planks 20 to 30cm long) by running cold water over them. Brush the salmon with the melted butter, sprinkle with mustard powder and season.

Put the cedar planks under the grill until they are smoking and giving off a fragrant cedar smell. Place three salmon portions on each plank, and replace under the grill. Cook for approximately 8 to 10 minutes without turning, until the salmon is lightly browned and medium rare.

To serve, place a portion of polenta on each plate and pour cider butter sauce around it. Place a portion of salmon on each plate, resting lightly on the polenta. Garnish with rocket leaves and a wedge of lemon.

blackened hapuku

with potato and goat's cheese purée and fresh mint slaw

potato and goat's cheese purée

1kg Agria potatoes

2 teaspoons salt

1 sprig thyme

1 bay leaf

½ cup cream

75gm unsalted butter

sea salt and freshly milled white pepper

200gm Chèvre de Bellay goat's cheese

blackened fish spice

1 tablespoon sea salt

3 tablespoons freshly milled white pepper

3 tablespoons freshly milled black pepper

3 tablespoons cayenne pepper

3 tablespoons whole fennel seeds

3 tablespoons mustard powder

1 tablespoon dried basil

1 tablespoon dried thyme

1 clove garlic, peeled, crushed and finely chopped

6 hapuku fillets, each approximately 200g

6 tablespoons melted butter

1 lemon, cut into 6 wedges

fresh mint slaw

3 cups loosely packed shredded cabbage

1 red chilli, seeds removed and sliced thinly

¼ cup fresh mint, loosely packed and coarsely chopped

1 teaspoon dried mint

sea salt and freshly milled black pepper

150ml lemon vinaigrette (recipe page 52)

Serves 6

I've been using this spice mix since 1989. Even when blackened fish is not on the menu, many customers still request fish cooked this way. If you would like the fish not quite as spicy, use less of the spice mix, but don't alter the ratios. To make this dish correctly you will need an extremely hot, heavy, cast-iron pan. When cooking this dish at Soul, we put two pans on to heat at 11.45am and leave them on full gas throughout the time we are cooking lunch. It doesn't damage the pans.

To make the purée, peel the potatoes and cover with cold water in a large saucepan. Add the salt, thyme and bay leaf, bring to the boil and simmer until tender (approximately 25 minutes).

Drain through a colander and discard the thyme and bay leaf. Mash the potato or pass it through a mouli.

Place the cream and butter in a saucepan and bring to the boil. Gradually stir in the mashed potato, a little at a time, to achieve a smooth, silky consistency. Season to taste. Crumble the goat's cheese and fold it into potato purée.

To make the spice mix, thoroughly combine the spices and herbs.

Heat a heavy, cast-iron pan until extremely hot. Dredge the fish fillets in the spice mix then shake off excess. Drizzle a tablespoon of melted butter on each piece of fish, and carefully place in the pan. A lot of smoke will appear, and maybe a small flame. Don't worry about the smoke, but don't inhale it. Blow out any flames, however, as they do taint the flavour of the fish.

Allow the spice coating to lightly blacken, then turn the fish. (Note: blackened does not mean burnt.) When using thick fish fillets, it may be necessary to take the pan from the heat to allow the fish to cook through once it has been turned. You can also put the pan in the oven for a few minutes to finish cooking the fish.

To make the slaw, toss the first five ingredients in a large bowl. Add the vinaigrette and toss again just before serving.

Serve the blackened fish on the mash with a wedge of lemon. A rocket salad or fresh mint slaw makes a great accompaniment. Blackened hapuku is also delicious served in a sandwich of warm ciabatta with this fresh mint slaw.

deep-fried blue cod

in beer batter with sauce gibriche

Although we refer to this fish as blue cod, Stephanie Alexander suggested to me that it isn't a cod at all. To gain clarification, I showed one to Mark Kurlansky, author of the book *Cod*. Stephanie was right! Apparently, a cod's large ventral fins are located under or in front of the pectorals, rather than behind them as with blue cod. So maybe we should call it faux cod.
Either way, everyone loves fish in batter and this batter truly is the best — light and crisp. It's great served with lemon wedges and maybe a dash of malt vinegar as well — a little habit I acquired from cooking in London in the '80s.

sauce gibriche

250g gherkins, roughly chopped

20g capers, roughly chopped

2 hard-boiled eggs, peeled and roughly chopped

1 cup flat-leaf parsley, roughly chopped and tightly packed

juice of half a lemon

3 dashes Tabasco sauce

pinch smoked paprika

1 portion mayonnaise (recipe page 135)

sea salt and freshly milled black or white pepper

beer batter

135g cornflour

135g self-raising flour

25ml vegetable oil

375ml beer

1 teaspoon salt

1½ litres vegetable oil for deep-frying

6 portions blue cod, each approximately 200g

flour for dusting

6 sprigs parsley

1 lemon, cut into wedges

Serves 6

To make the sauce, fold the roughly chopped ingredients, lemon juice, Tabasco sauce and paprika into the mayonnaise, and season to taste.

To make the batter, whisk all the ingredients together and pass through a sieve to eliminate any lumps.

To cook the cod, heat the vegetable oil in a heavy-based saucepan. Dust the fish with a little flour and shake off any excess. In batches, dip the cod in the batter, removing as much excess batter as possible by running your fingers down the fillet, and cook for approximately 4 minutes, turning if necessary, until golden brown. Remove from pan and place on absorbent paper to drain.

Arrange the fish on plates and garnish with parsley deep-fried in oil for 30 seconds, lemon wedges and a side dish of sauce gibriche.

roast hapuku

on parsnip skordalia, broccolini and parsley salad with tomato pomegranate dressing

tomato pomegranate dressing

¾ tablespoon pomegranate molasses

8 whole shallots, peeled and finely chopped

2 cloves garlic, peeled and finely chopped

juice of 2 lemons

4 fresh tomatoes, deseeded and cut into 0.5cm dice

375ml extra virgin olive oil

salt and freshly milled black pepper

parsnip skordalia

500g parsnips

500ml milk

½ teaspoon salt

juice and zest of 2 lemons

2 cloves garlic, peeled, then crushed with salt

25g fresh breadcrumbs

100ml extra virgin olive oil

sea salt and freshly milled white pepper

broccolini and parsley salad

8 strips streaky bacon

1 tablespoon extra virgin olive oil

8 cups broccolini

4 cups flat-leaf parsley leaves, tightly packed

2 red onions, peeled and finely sliced

sea salt and freshly milled black pepper

2 tablespoons olive oil (not extra virgin)

½ tablespoon butter

6 portions hapuku, each approximately 200g

Serves 6

To make the dressing, place molasses, shallots, garlic, lemon juice, tomatoes and olive oil in a bowl and whisk together well. Season to taste.

To make the skordalia, core the parsnips and cut into 3cm cubes. Place in a heavy-based saucepan and cover with the milk. Bring to the boil, reduce the heat and simmer for 10 to 15 minutes until very soft.

Place the parsnips and milk into a food processor with the salt, lemon juice and zest, garlic and breadcrumbs and process until smooth. Continue to process, slowly drizzling in the olive oil until it is all incorporated. Season to taste and allow to cool.

To prepare the salad, cut the bacon into batons and fry in the oil until crispy. Put to one side on absorbent paper. Place the broccolini in a saucepan of simmering water and cook until tender. Remove and place in an ice bath to cool. Drain and pat dry with absorbent paper.

Cut the broccolini into strips lengthwise and combine with the parsley leaves, red onion and bacon. Season to taste.

Toss the salad with the dressing and set aside.

To cook the fish heat either 1 or 2 large heavy based frypans depending on size of fish.

Heat the oil until smoking, add the knob of butter and place the fish presentation side down in pan. Cook on high until golden brown, turn the fish, reduce heat and continue cooking for a further 4 minutes or until fish is just cooked.

To serve, spoon skordalia onto plates, arrange salad on top then place a piece of hapuku on top of the salad.

john dory

on parsnip mash with lentil, shallot and olive vinaigrette

In London John Dory is called 'poor man's turbot'. I disagree. John Dory was the first fish I cooked as an apprentice chef and I enjoy it as much now as I did then. This dish is fast becoming a classic at Soul, especially in autumn and winter, when the first frosts really sweeten the parsnips. The golden ras el hanout is one of Greg Malouf's fantastic spice mixes.

golden ras el hanout

2 teaspoons coriander seeds

2 teaspoons cumin seeds

2 teaspoons turmeric

½ teaspoon chilli powder

1 teaspoon ground ginger

lentil, shallot and olive vinaigrette

1 cup cooked puy lentils

½ cup finely chopped shallots

3 tablespoons pitted and sliced kalamata olives

2 teaspoons fresh thyme leaves

½ cup diced tomatoes (flesh only), deseeded

3 tablespoons chopped flat-leaf parsley

¼ cup extra virgin olive oil

1 tablespoon sherry vinegar

juice of 1 lemon

sea salt and freshly milled black pepper

6 fillets John Dory, each approximately 180g, skin off

3 tablespoons grapeseed oil

1 tablespoon unsalted butter

1 portion parsnip mash (recipe page 73)

Serves 6

Preheat the oven to 180°C.

To make the ras el hanout, roast the coriander and cumin seeds for 3 to 4 minutes in a pan in the oven (do not burn). Remove from oven and grind into a fine powder. Sieve together with the other spices.

To prepare the vinaigrette, combine the lentils, shallots, olives, thyme, tomato and parsley. In another bowl, whisk together the oil and vinegar and add the lemon juice. Add to the lentil mixture and season to taste.

Place the lentil mixture into a heatproof bowl and warm gently over a saucepan of simmering water for 5 to 6 minutes. Taste to check the seasoning and add a little more lemon juice, and/or salt and pepper if required.

Lightly season both sides of the fish fillets with the ras el hanout (remember the spice mix is playing a supporting role, not masking the delicate flavour of this fish).

Heat a frypan over a medium to high heat. Add the grapeseed oil and lower to a medium heat. Add the fillets and cook for 2 to 3 minutes before turning carefully with a spatula. Add butter and cook for a further 2 minutes.

To serve, heat the parsnip mash and spoon a portion into the middle of each of six large plates. Carefully lift the fish fillets from the frypan and place one on top of each portion of the mash. Spoon the lentil vinaigrette over the fish, letting a little fall onto the plate.

grilled snapper

with coriander and walnut vinaigrette on sage-fried potatoes

coriander and walnut vinaigrette

1½ cups coriander leaves, loosely packed

¼ cup mint leaves

1 tablespoon deseeded and finely chopped red chilli

¼ red onion, peeled and finely chopped

¾ cup walnuts, toasted and coarsely chopped

6 tablespoons extra virgin olive oil

1½ tablespoons freshly squeezed lemon juice

1½ teaspoons pomegranate molasses

salt and freshly milled black pepper

sage-fried potatoes

½ cup grapeseed oil

900g gourmet potatoes, cooked with skin on, cut in half

½ cup sage leaves, loosely packed

yoghurt tahini dressing

150ml yoghurt

3 tablespoons tahini

1 clove garlic, peeled and crushed

juice of 1 lemon

3 dashes Tabasco sauce

sea salt and freshly milled white pepper

6 snapper fillets, each approximately 200g, skin on and scaled

sea salt and freshly milled white pepper

1 teaspoon sumac (optional)

Serves 6

This is a Greg Malouf recipe from when he first consulted to Soul in 2002. It is so good that I very much doubt we will ever take it off the menu.

To make the vinaigrette, coarsely chop the coriander and mint and mix with the chilli, red onion and walnuts. In another bowl whisk together the oil, juice and molasses and season to taste.

To prepare the potatoes, heat the grapeseed oil in a sauté pan over a high heat. Add the pre-cooked potatoes and sauté for 5 to 8 minutes. Sprinkle with the sage and cook for a further 3 minutes until the potatoes are golden brown.

To make the yoghurt dressing, combine all ingredients in a bowl and whisk until smooth. Season to taste.

To cook the snapper, season the fillets and grill for approximately 3 minutes on each side. (The cooking time will vary depending on the thickness of the fillets.)

To serve, combine the coriander and walnut mix with the vinaigrette and season to taste. Place a serving of sage potatoes in the middle of each of six large plates. Arrange the snapper fillets on top and cover with the coriander and walnut vinaigrette and some yoghurt tahini dressing.

At Soul we finish the dish by sprinkling it with sumac (a Middle Eastern spice with citrus flavours).

roast hapuku

over cannellini beans, fennel and rocket salad with celery salsa verde

This dish was inspired by a trip to San Francisco with Peter Thornley. We ate a similar dish that was prepared and cooked while we sat up at the kitchen counter and watched the chefs going hell-for-leather in an open kitchen right in front of us. No waiters were required; the chefs just passed the food over when it was ready. What a great cooking lesson! Here we have sought to recreate that meal using tender, creamy cannellini beans and roasted hapuku, wild rocket and shaved fennel.

cannellini beans

1 cup cannellini beans

3 cups vegetable stock

1 small carrot, quartered

1 small onion, peeled and halved

1 clove garlic, peeled

2 sprigs thyme

1 bay leaf

sea salt

2 tablespoons extra virgin olive oil

lemon dressing

1 clove garlic, peeled

½ red chilli, seeds removed

3 tablespoons lemon juice

150ml extra virgin olive oil

sea salt and freshly milled white pepper

hapuku

6 portions hapuku, each approximately 200g

sea salt and freshly milled white pepper

4 tablespoons extra virgin olive oil

3 tablespoons butter

6 sprigs thyme

fennel and rocket salad

3 medium-size heads fennel, thinly sliced

100g wild rocket

6 tablespoons celery salsa verde (recipe page 134)

Rinse the beans under cold running water. Place in a saucepan and cover with vegetable stock. Bring to a simmer over a medium heat and skim off any foam that appears on the surface.

Give the beans a good stir and add the carrot, onion, garlic, thyme and bay leaf. Reduce heat and simmer gently, uncovered, for 1 to 2 hours, depending on how fresh and dry the beans are. Stir occasionally to ensure the beans at the bottom do not get crushed, and add more stock if necessary.

To check if they are done, place a few beans in a little of the liquid in the refrigerator for a couple of minutes, then taste. The beans are cooked if they are tender and there is no starchy taste.

Remove saucepan from the heat and season with sea salt. Taste the cooking liquor, not the beans as it will take some time for the beans to absorb the salt. Stir in the olive oil.

For the lemon dressing, crush the garlic and chilli with a little salt in a mortar and pestle. Whisk together with the lemon juice in a bowl. Add the oil in a steady stream, whisking to combine. Season to taste. Set aside until required.

Preheat the oven to 200°C. To cook the hapuku, heat an ovenproof frypan over a medium to high heat. Season both sides of the fillets. Add the oil to the pan, reduce the heat and place the fish gently into the pan. Cook for 3 minutes, then turn with a spatula and cook the other side for 1 further minute. Add the butter and thyme and place the pan in the oven for 3 to 4 minutes, depending on the thickness of the fillets. Baste two or three times with the roasting juices.

To serve, spoon the beans into warm bowls with a little of the cooking liquor. Toss the fennel and wild rocket with a little lemon dressing and place on top of the beans.

Remove hapuku from the oven, lift from the frypan and rest gently on the salad. Deglaze the frying pan with the remaining lemon dressing and spoon over the fish. Place a spoonful of the celery salsa verde on top of the fish.

pasta & risotto

scampi

wild rocket and vanilla bean risotto

This is a Bill Marchetti risotto that we had on the menu at Ramses.

3 vanilla pods

150g butter

risotto base (recipe page 137)

juice of 1 lemon

18 scampi, peeled

100g wild rocket

6 tablespoons freshly grated parmesan cheese

sea salt and freshly milled white pepper

Serves 6

Split the vanilla pods lengthwise and scrape the seeds into the butter. Beat with a wooden spoon or in a food processor to make a rich vanilla butter. Set aside at room temperature.

Make the risotto base. Taste the rice to make sure it is perfectly cooked. Add the lemon juice.

Fold the scampi and rocket into the risotto. Fold through the vanilla butter and parmesan. Season to taste. Serve immediately.

crisp duck confit

with gnocchi and braised winter greens

aromatic salt

½ cup sea salt

zest of 1 orange

zest of ½ lemon

40g root ginger

1 teaspoon whole coriander seeds

¼ cinnamon quill

6 cloves garlic, peeled

3 white and 3 black peppercorns

1 star anise

duck

6 duck legs

5–7 cups duck fat

duck sauce

250g duck bones

2 tablespoons unsalted butter

½ cup shallots, peeled and chopped

1 clove garlic, peeled

1 cup red wine

2 sprigs thyme

¼ cinnamon stick

½ cup golden chicken stock
(recipe page 139)

2 cups reduced golden chicken
stock (recipe page 139)

3 tablespoons grapeseed oil

½ portion potato gnocchi
(recipe page 137)

2 tablespoons unsalted butter

sea salt and freshly milled white
pepper

½ portion braised winter greens
(recipe page 76)

Serves 6

For the aromatic salt mix together all the ingredients and grind in a spice grinder until the mixture is well combined. Set aside.

Rinse the duck legs under cold running water and pat dry with absorbent paper. Trim off any excess fat.

Rub ½ tablespoon of aromatic salt into each leg, paying attention to the joint and thicker areas. Place legs on a tray in a single layer, cover with cling film and refrigerate for 24 hours.

To make the confit, heat the oven to 130°C. Rinse the duck legs well under cold running water and dry thoroughly with absorbent paper. Lay the legs in a heavy casserole dish just large enough to hold them in a single layer.

Melt the duck fat and pour over the legs to a depth of 2cm above the duck. Place the casserole in the oven and cook for 8 to 9 hours.

Remove casserole from the oven and check the duck legs are cooked by inserting a small knife into the meat. It should be very tender and just start pulling off the bone with ease. Do not over-cook the duck, or the meat will fall apart when being crisped.

Allow to cool with the legs still in the fat. When cool, gently lift the legs from the casserole and place in a smaller container. Pour over the fat to totally cover the legs. Cover the container and keep in the refrigerator for up to 2 weeks.

For the sauce, heat the oven to 180°C. Roast the duck bones until golden (approximately 12 to 15 minutes).

In a saucepan, melt the butter over a medium heat. Add the shallots and garlic and sauté until lightly coloured.

Add the browned duck bones and sauté for a further 2 to 3 minutes. Add the red wine and reduce by three quarters. Add the thyme, cinnamon and both chicken stocks. Simmer gently for 15 to 20 minutes to sauce consistency.

Strain the sauce through a wet-muslin-lined chinois. Repeat if necessary until the sauce contains no debris. Do not force the sauce through the chinois or the sauce will become cloudy.

Cover the sauce with a paper lid (cartouche) and keep warm until required.

To crisp, heat the oven to 200°C. Remove the duck legs from the fat and wipe off any excess. Place in a roasting dish in a single layer, skin-side up. Put into the oven for 12 to 15 minutes, basting with the fat from the legs as it melts. The legs should become crisp and golden.

Heat a non-stick frypan over a medium to high heat and add the grapeseed oil. Add the gnocchi and sauté for 1 minute. Reduce heat to medium and continue to sauté gnocchi for a further 4 minutes until golden brown. Add butter and sauté for 1 more minute. Season to taste.

To serve, place the gnocchi in the middle of each plate and top with a neat pile of winter greens. Rest the crisp duck on the greens, and drizzle the sauce over.

chilli squid

prawn and cucumber risotto

I love this risotto because the cucumber juice keeps it fresh and crisp on the palate. You can make the risotto base from scratch, using cucumber juice instead of the chicken stock.

3 large telegraph cucumbers

2 tablespoons extra virgin olive oil

400g squid, thinly sliced

300g prawns, shells removed

2 tablespoons peeled and finely chopped shallot

3 teaspoons finely chopped red chilli

risotto base (recipe page 137)

2 tablespoons unsalted butter

6 tablespoons grated parmesan

¼ cup fresh coriander, loosely packed

juice of 1 lime

sea salt and freshly milled white pepper

Serves 6

Peel cucumbers, and liquidise in a food processor or blender. Strain through a fine sieve or squeeze through a muslin cloth. This should yield approximately 1 litre of light green juice.

Heat the olive oil in a saucepan and sauté squid and prawns for 1 to 2 minutes. Remove from the pan and set aside to keep warm. Without washing the pan, add shallots and chillies and cook for 1 to 2 minutes. (Add a little more oil if necessary.)

Add the risotto base and enough cucumber juice to just cover the rice. Bring to the boil and simmer until the rice has absorbed all the juice.

Fold in the butter, parmesan, prawns, squid, coriander and lime juice. Season and serve immediately.

ilam hardy potato **tortellini** with poached scallops

tortellini

500g Ilam hardy potatoes, peeled and diced

4 sprigs thyme

1 bay leaf

2 tablespoons cream

25g unsalted butter

sea salt and freshly milled white pepper

30 gozo dumpling wrappers

1 beaten egg white for brushing

poached scallops

500ml sweetcorn nage (recipe page 135)

75g fresh sweetcorn kernels, cut from cob

150g unsalted butter, diced

sea salt and freshly milled white pepper

1 teaspoon peanut or vegetable oil

30 fresh scallops

Serves 6

To make the tortellini, place the potatoes, half of the thyme and the bay leaf in a large saucepan of boiling, salted water. Cook until tender.

Drain well, removing bay leaf and thyme. Mash or pass potato through a mouli.

Warm the cream and butter together, and gradually stir into the potato to achieve a light, smooth consistency. Season to taste, and allow to cool.

Place the sweetcorn nage in a saucepan with the sweetcorn kernels and reduce by 50 per cent. Whisk in the diced butter until amalgamated. Season to taste.

Pick the leaves from the remaining two thyme sprigs and add to the sauce.

To fill the tortellini, lay out the gozo wrappers on the bench. Brush each with a little egg white, and place a dessertspoon of the potato filling on each wrapper. Fold over wrappers to enclose the filling and press edges together to seal.

Cook the tortellini in boiling, salted water until al dente (3 to 4 minutes).

Simmer the nage gently for 1 to 2 minutes. Meanwhile, heat the vegetable oil in a heavy-based frypan. When the oil is smoking sear the scallops in the pan for 1 to 2 minutes. Remove from the pan. For 30 scallops you may need to do this in 2 batches or use 2 frypans at the same time.

Drain the tortellini and arrange five in each bowl. Top each tortellini with a scallop.

Spoon the sweetcorn kernels in the sauce over and around the tortellini.

Froth the remaining nage with a whiz stick or hand blender and spoon bubbly sauce over and around the tortellini.

risotto
with mushrooms

This recipe uses porcini mushrooms, called ceps in France. In New Zealand they are only available dried, which concentrates the flavour so much that porcini are used almost like a seasoning. They are also very expensive.

Dried porcini must be reconstituted in warm to hot water for 15 to 20 minutes before use. Keep the soaking water, which will be dark brown and intensely flavoured.

5g dried porcini mushrooms

¼ cup extra virgin olive oil

500g flat mushrooms, thickly sliced

1 clove garlic, peeled and sliced

2 tablespoons chopped basil

juice of ½ lemon

risotto base (recipe page 137)

2½ cups chicken stock (recipe page 138)

½ cup cubed unsalted butter, room temperature

½ cup parmesan cheese, freshly grated

sea salt and freshly milled black pepper

Serves 6

Put the dried porcini mushrooms in a small bowl and just cover with warm water. Set aside for 20 minutes. Remove the reconstituted porcini, roughly chop and set aside. Retain soaking water for use in the risotto.

In a stainless steel saucepan, heat the oil until smoking. Add the mushrooms and garlic and fry, stirring constantly, for 15 to 20 minutes or until the mushrooms have become very dark. (Add a little water if the mushrooms become too dry.) Add basil and lemon juice. Remove mushroom mixture from saucepan and set aside to keep warm.

To the same pan, add the risotto base and enough chicken stock to just cover the rice. Add the liquid from the porcini. Simmer until the rice has absorbed most of the liquid and is cooked perfectly.

Fold in the butter in small pieces, the mushroom mixture, porcini, parmesan, salt and pepper. Do not over-stir. Serve immediately.

soul bar & bistro

salads & starters

crispy potato
and goat's cheese terrine with rocket salad and lemon vinaigrette

This dish has appeared on many menus over the past five years, mainly as an accompaniment to lamb rack. It is also great served with a rocket salad as a lunch dish, as described here.
The French goat's cheese has a higher fat content and is slightly softer. This adds a richness which can't be achieved with feta alone.
This dish is for my sister who, due to her love of potatoes, was nick-named 'Spud Watson'.

terrine

250g sliced streaky bacon

1.1kg potatoes, peeled and thinly sliced

150g Camembert cheese, sliced

150g Chèvre de Bellay goat's cheese, thinly sliced

½ cup chopped sage leaves

salt and freshly milled pepper

lemon vinaigrette

1 clove garlic, peeled

½ red chilli, deseeded

3 tablespoons lemon juice

150ml extra virgin olive oil

sea salt and freshly milled white pepper

rocket salad

3 cups rocket

Serves 6

Preheat the oven to 190°C.

To assemble the terrine, lightly grease a terrine mould or loaf tin and line with strips of bacon, leaving enough bacon hanging over the edges to fold over and cover the top. Fill the mould with alternating thin layers of potato, Camembert, goat's cheese and sage, seasoning each layer with salt and pepper and pressing down firmly as you go.

Build up the terrine to 5cm above the top of the mould and fold over excess bacon. Cover with tinfoil.

Place the terrine in a roasting dish and fill the dish with boiling water to halfway up the mould. Place a weight such as a brick on top. Bake in the oven for 3 hours.

Remove from the oven and cool, keeping the weight on top.

To make the dressing, crush the garlic and chilli with a little salt in a mortar and pestle. Whisk into the lemon juice in a bowl. Add the olive oil in a steady stream and continue to whisk to combine. Season to taste.

To assemble, turn the cooled terrine out of the mould and cut into 3cm-thick slices.

Lightly dust the slices with flour and pan-fry in a little oil over a medium heat until golden brown and warm all the way through. Serve on a rocket salad dressed with lemon vinaigrette.

tuna tartare two ways

1

600g big eye tuna (cut into 1cm neat dice)

1 tablespoon truffle oil

120g Puhoi goat's feta

3 teaspoons finely chopped chives

3 pears, ripe but firm, cut into 5cm batons

6 leaves rocket, julienned

dressing

1 tablespoon extra virgin olive oil

3 tablespoon grapeseed oil

1 tablespoon truffle oil

2 tablespoons mirin

½ teaspoon sake

freshly milled white pepper

Maldon sea salt

½ teaspoon champagne vinegar

Serves 6

I love this tartare with pears and truffle oil, but I also love tuna tartare with green olive compote, so I've included that recipe too. It was far too hard to choose between them.

Splash the tuna with the truffle oil. Gently fold through the diced feta and chopped chives. Divide the mixture into six portions and push each portion, one at a time, into a 12cm pastry ring so it sits flat on the plate.

To make the dressing, combine all ingredients and season to taste.

Toss the sliced pears in half of the dressing. Make a neat pile of pear batons on top of each tartare. Spoon the remaining dressing over and around the tartare, and sit one julienned leaf of rocket neatly on top of the pears on each tartare.

2

600g fresh big eye tuna, cut into 1cm neat dice, mixed with 3 tablespoons extra virgin olive oil and seasoned with salt and pepper

1 loaf ciabatta, toasted under a grill or on a barbeque

green olive compote

1 ½ cups Gaeta green olives (in their own juice)

2 Ortiz anchovies

2 teaspoons capers

2 tablespoons lemon oil

zest of two limes

¼ cup flat-leaf parsley, stems removed

sea salt and freshly milled pepper

Serves 6

Remove the stones from the olives. Combine olive flesh with the other compote ingredients in a food processor and roughly chop. Season to taste. Divide the mixture into six and pile tuna into the centre of six large plates. Top each pile with a tablespoon of olive compote. Serve with toasted ciabatta slices.

chOpped salad with blue cheese dressing

blue cheese dressing

⅓ cup mayonnaise (recipe page 135)

⅓ cup sour cream

⅓ cup blue cheese (at room temperature)

2 tablespoons hot water

salt and freshly milled pepper to taste

dash of Tabasco sauce to taste

salad

1 cup green cabbage

1 cup radicchio

2 cups rocket

3 cups cos lettuce

1 cup spinach

Serves 6

To make the dressing, place all the dairy products in a blender. Blend at low speed, adding hot water, a little at a time, until it forms a dressing consistency.

Season to taste with salt, pepper and Tabasco sauce.

To make the salad, wash all the leaves and pat dry with absorbent paper. Roughly chop the leaves into small pieces.

To serve, place all the greens in a large bowl and gently fold in the blue cheese dressing until the leaves are well coated. Partly fill six medium-sized shallow bowls, forming the leaves into a loose cone shape in each bowl, with the leaves as high as possible.

A very American-style salad, inspired by a visit there. It has proven amazingly popular at Soul. The exact combination of leaves is not really all that important, but use a mixture of hardy leaves, like cos, and some soft leaves, like rocket. If you use too many soft leaves the salad will collapse.

roasted beets

with orange, fennel and ricotta salad

beets

600g baby beets

2 tablespoons extra virgin olive oil

3 sprigs thyme

1 bay leaf

2 teaspoons water

dressing

zest and juice of 2 oranges

3 tablespoons extra virgin olive oil

4 tablespoons walnut oil

1 tablespoon grapeseed oil

3 teaspoons cabernet sauvignon vinegar

salt and freshly milled black pepper

salad

3 oranges, peeled and segmented

120g fennel (three bulbs), thinly sliced

150g Zany Zeus ricotta

100g rocket

100g watercress

Serves 6

Preheat the oven to 180°C.

Top and tail the beets and place in an oven dish with the olive oil, thyme, bay leaf and water. Cover with foil and bake for 40 minutes until soft. Remove from the oven and cool. The skins can be rubbed off at this stage or left on as desired.

To make the dressing, whisk together all the ingredients in a bowl and season to taste.

Halve the beets and season. Toss with a little of the dressing.

Divide the beets into six portions, placing each portion in the middle of a large round plate. Lay the orange segments on top of the beets.

Toss the fennel with a little dressing, salt and pepper and then lay it on top of the beets and orange. Crumble the ricotta on top.

Toss the rocket and watercress with a little dressing and some salt to taste. Arrange the dressed salad leaves on top of each serving.

Sometimes I have phases where I eat the same things every day. I am currently eating this salad at least four times a week. The ricotta we use is from a new supplier — look out for it because it's beautifully light in texture, and what a great name: Zany Zeus.

pukekohe onion tarts

with goat's cheese, fig and endive salad and honeyed sichuan hazelnuts

This tart makes a superb lunch or vegetarian starter. At present it appears on the Soul menu as an accompaniment to grilled beef fillet.

3 large Pukekohe onions

12 sprigs thyme

6 teaspoons brown sugar

6 tablespoons unsalted butter

6 puff-pastry discs, each 10cm in diameter

180g Mount Hector goat's cheese, divided into 6 portions

goat's cheese, fig and endive salad

¼ cup hazelnuts

1 tablespoon peanut oil

2 tablespoons honey

½ teaspoon Sichuan peppercorns, crushed

5 tablespoons extra virgin olive oil

2 tablespoons grapeseed oil

3 tablespoons fig vincotta

1 tablespoon cabernet vinegar

3 (endive) witloof

sea salt and freshly milled black pepper

Serves 6

Preheat the oven to 180°C.

Cut the onions in half horizontally, trim each half to a 3cm thick slice and remove the root. Strip the leaves from the thyme sprigs.

Place the brown sugar, butter and thyme leaves in a galette pan and melt over a medium heat.

Place the onion halves cut-surface down on a chopping board and cover each one with a circle of pastry, moulding it with your hands around the onion.

Place each pastry-covered onion into the galette pan, pastry-side up, and bake in the oven for 25 to 30 minutes. Insert a skewer into the middle of each onion tart to check if it is cooked — the onion should feel soft.

Roast the hazelnuts in a hot oven for 8 to 10 minutes, then tip into a clean towel and rub off the skins.

Heat the peanut oil in a non-stick frypan. Add hazelnuts and toss for 1 minute. Add the honey and caramelise the nuts, then sprinkle in the peppercorns.

Remove from the heat and pour onto a sheet of greaseproof paper to cool, then crush with the back of a knife until the nuts resemble coarse gravel.

For the dressing, whisk together the olive oil, grapeseed oil, vincotta and cabernet vinegar. Season to taste.

Separate the witloof into individual leaves. Toss with the hazelnuts and 2 tablespoons of the dressing.

To serve, turn out the onion tarts. Place a slice of Mount Hector cheese in the middle of each tart and return to the oven for 1 minute to warm.

Remove tarts from oven. Arrange some salad neatly on each plate. Set tarts near the edge of each plate and spoon around the extra dressing.

seared scallops

on toasted wheat and cranberry pilaf with lime and coconut froth

apple curry oil

1 cup grapeseed oil

½ cup diced apple

½ cup diced carrot

1 clove garlic

¼ cup diced onion

2 tablespoons mild curry powder

1 teaspoon ground turmeric

1 teaspoon ground cumin

4 cups water

1 teaspoon salt

1 cup ebly

2 tablespoons peanut oil

½ cup dried cranberries

sea salt and freshly milled white pepper

420g scallops, roes removed

lime and coconut froth

1 cup coconut cream

¼ teaspoon green curry paste

1 kaffir lime leaf, julienned

25g root ginger, julienned

juice of 2 limes

garnish

1 kaffir lime leaf, julienned

25gm root ginger, julienned and blanched in boiling water for 2 minutes then refreshed in cold water. Drain and reserve for garnishing.

Serves 6

Make the apple curry oil 1 to 2 hours in advance. Heat 2 tablespoons of the grapeseed oil in a saucepan and sweat the apple, carrot, garlic and onion until soft. Add the spices and cook over a low heat for 4 to 5 minutes. Pour in the remaining oil and bring to a gentle simmer for 5 minutes.

Remove from the heat and allow to infuse for 30 minutes, then purée thoroughly with a whiz stick.

Pass the oil through a muslin-lined sieve and allow to filter for 1 to 2 hours. Store in a covered container in the refrigerator.

In a medium-size saucepan bring the water to the boil. Add the salt, then the ebly and cook until tender (approximately 10 minutes). Drain and spread on a tray to cool.

To make the lime and coconut froth, place the coconut cream, curry paste, lime leaf and ginger in a saucepan. Bring to a simmer for 3 to 4 minutes and add the lime juice. Do not allow it to boil.

Pour the liquid through a fine sieve to remove any debris, and keep warm without boiling.

To serve, heat the peanut oil in a large non-stick frypan. Add the ebly and toast until it is a light-golden colour (approximately 4 minutes). Take care, as the ebly pops like popcorn. Add the cranberries and toss together. Season to taste.

Season the scallops. Heat a non-stick frypan and sear the scallops for 30 seconds on each side.

Spoon a portion of the ebly and cranberry mixture into the middle of each serving plate and arrange the scallops on top.

Using a whiz stick, froth the sauce until large bubbles appear. Spoon over the scallops.

Drizzle each serving with a little apple curry oil and top with 3 to 4 strips of the julienned lime leaf and ginger.

silverbeet and caramelised onion tart with tarragon tzatziki

Greg Malouf introduced this dish to Soul. We make it in individual pans but it can be made as one large tart. At Soul, we also make it in tiny pies for cocktail parties.

tarragon tzatziki

800g unsweetened, natural yoghurt

1 clove garlic, peeled

1 cup grated cucumber, skin on

juice of 1 lemon

2 teaspoons dried mint

2 tablespoons chopped fresh tarragon

salt and freshly milled black pepper

2 tablespoons chopped parsley

caramelised onions

2 red onions, peeled and thinly sliced

100ml port

filling

30ml olive oil

1 onion, peeled and finely diced

1 clove garlic, peeled and finely chopped

1 red chilli, deseeded and finely chopped

1 kg silverbeet, stalks cut into 1cm dice, leaves ripped into pieces approximately 5cm x 5cm

1 ½ teaspoons allspice

85ml freshly squeezed lemon juice

100ml white wine

salt and freshly ground black pepper

300g Bulgarian feta, cut into 3cm cubes

pastry

150g clarified butter

16 sheets filo pastry

Serves 8

Preheat the oven to 200°C.

To make the tzaztiki, put the yoghurt in a muslin cloth to drain overnight in the fridge. Crush the garlic with some salt. Once the yoghurt is well drained, mix in the rest of the ingredients and season to taste.

To caramelise the onions, place them and the port in a heavy-based saucepan and simmer for approximately 10 minutes until the onions are soft and caramelised. Set to one side.

To make the filling, heat the olive oil in a large, deep, heavy-based saucepan. Sweat the onion, garlic and chilli over a medium heat until soft.

Add the diced silverbeet stalks and cook until tender. Add the allspice, lemon juice and white wine and cook over medium to high heat until most of the liquid has been absorbed or evaporated, stirring frequently.

Stir through the silverbeet leaves in stages, keeping the mixture moving. Reduce down any further liquid, cooking silverbeet until it is very wilted.

Pour the mixture into a colander or sieve and drain off any excess liquid. Place to one side and cool. Once cooled, stir through the cubed feta.

To prepare the pastry, melt the clarified butter. Lay out 4 sheets of the filo pastry so that half of each sheet overlaps, to make a large square. Stick sheets together by brushing with the clarified butter. Repeat so the square is four layers thick.

Butter a 22cm-diameter round baking tin and place on a flat tray. Line with the filo pastry, letting the extra pastry fall outside the edge.

Fill with the silverbeet mixture and fold the excess pastry over the top to enclose the filling. Brush with butter.

Place another flat tray on top and flip the tart over. Butter the new top side of the tart. Bake for 30 minutes.

Serve with a few green leaves, like watercress or rocket, and a spoonful of tarragon tzatziki.

soul's seafood chowder

100g unsalted butter

100g peeled and chopped onion

100g peeled and chopped carrot

100g chopped celery

100g chopped leek

1 clove garlic, peeled and finely chopped

2 threads saffron

100g plain flour

1.25 litres fish stock, hot

150ml milk

2 tablespoons each chopped parsley, dill, oregano, marjoram or basil

100g whole-kernel corn

sea salt and freshly milled white pepper

200ml cream

600g fresh white fish, cut into 2cm dice, eg snapper, tarakihi, flounder, gurnard

300g mussels, steamed and removed from shells

100g shrimps, defrosted (or fresh if available)

2 tablespoons chopped parsley

Serves 10

Melt the butter in a large saucepan. Add the onion, carrot, celery, leek, garlic and saffron. Cook without colouring until soft (approximately 8 to 10 minutes). Remove from heat, add the flour and mix well. Return to heat and gradually add hot stock, then the milk. Bring to the boil and simmer for 20 minutes, stirring occasionally, then add the chopped herbs and sweetcorn and season to taste.

Add the cream, fish, mussels and shrimps. Simmer for 5 to 10 minutes to cook the fish, then serve in deep bowls, sprinkled with chopped parsley.

The base can be stored in the fridge or freezer and reheated when required. Bring to a simmer before adding the cream, fish and shellfish.

This is not really a chowder, but it is an extremely popular fish soup nonetheless. It appeared on the menu at Ramses and Soul, and we rarely make less than 40 litres of it per week. My father, Gerald, always orders this dish.

sweetcorn soup with fresh crayfish and parsley pesto

sweetcorn soup

1.5kg fresh sweetcorn (8 cobs)

2.5 litres fish stock

8 bay leaves

50g unsalted butter

50g shallots, peeled and finely chopped

1 whole red chilli

salt and freshly milled white pepper

parsley pesto

1 cup flat-leaf parsley leaves, well packed

3 tablespoons toasted pine nuts

2 cloves garlic, peeled and crushed

juice of 1 lemon

½ cup extra virgin olive oil

salt and freshly milled black pepper

200g crayfish meat

Serves 8

Cut kernels off the cobs and set aside. In a large saucepan, cover the cobs with the fish stock, adding the bay leaves. Bring to the boil and simmer for 20 minutes.

In a separate large pan, melt the butter and sweat the shallots and chilli for 5 minutes. Add the corn kernels and cook for a further 5 minutes.

Strain the stock and pour over the kernels, shallots and chilli. Simmer for 15 minutes.

Purée with a whiz stick or in a food processor. Pass through a fine sieve or strainer. Season to taste.

To make the pesto, blend the parsley, pine nuts, garlic and lemon juice in a food processor until smooth. Blend in the olive oil and season to taste.

To serve, place 25g of crayfish in the bottom of eight large bowls. Pour in the hot soup and drizzle with the pesto.

tea petal-rubbed akaroa salmon
rhubarb and orange salad with mirin and sake dressing

Akaroa salmon is without doubt New Zealand's finest – farmed in the deep, natural waters of Akaroa harbour. The farm's owner, Tom Bates, is passionate about his salmon. I first tried his fish at a lunch during a chef's conference in Christchurch in the 1990s. I've never looked back – it's a true quality product.

2 ½ tablespoons brown sugar, firmly packed

1 tablespoon sea salt

¼ teaspoon ground tea flowers

420g Akaroa salmon fillet, skinned and boned

rhubarb and orange salad

200g rhubarb

25g castor sugar

good pinch sea salt

2 oranges, peeled and segmented

mirin and sake dressing

¼ cup walnut oil

2 tablespoons mirin

1 tablespoon sake

1 tablespoon rice wine vinegar

1 tablespoon grapeseed oil

1 tablespoon extra virgin olive oil

2 tablespoons orange juice

sea salt and freshly milled white pepper

garnish

1 tablespoon chopped chives

Serves 6

Prepare the rub by combining the brown sugar, salt and ground tea flowers. Rub this mixture into both sides of the salmon fillet. Wrap it in cling film and place in the refrigerator for 1 to 2 hours, but no longer.

Slice the rhubarb thinly on an angle. Sprinkle with the sugar and sea salt and allow to stand in a sieve for 4 to 5 minutes until the rhubarb becomes a little limp. Gently pat dry with absorbent paper.

For the dressing, combine the first seven ingredients in a bowl and whisk until well combined. Season to taste.

Remove the salmon from the refrigerator and unwrap gently. Wipe off the rub and pat dry. Cut the fillet in half lengthwise. Slice each half into nine 1cm-thick slices.

To serve, gently fold together the orange segments and the rhubarb with a little of the dressing. Place a serving of salad in the middle of each plate; and three slices of salmon on top. Spoon the remaining dressing over and around the salmon. Sprinkle with chopped chives. A selection of small salad leaves may also be placed on top of the salmon.

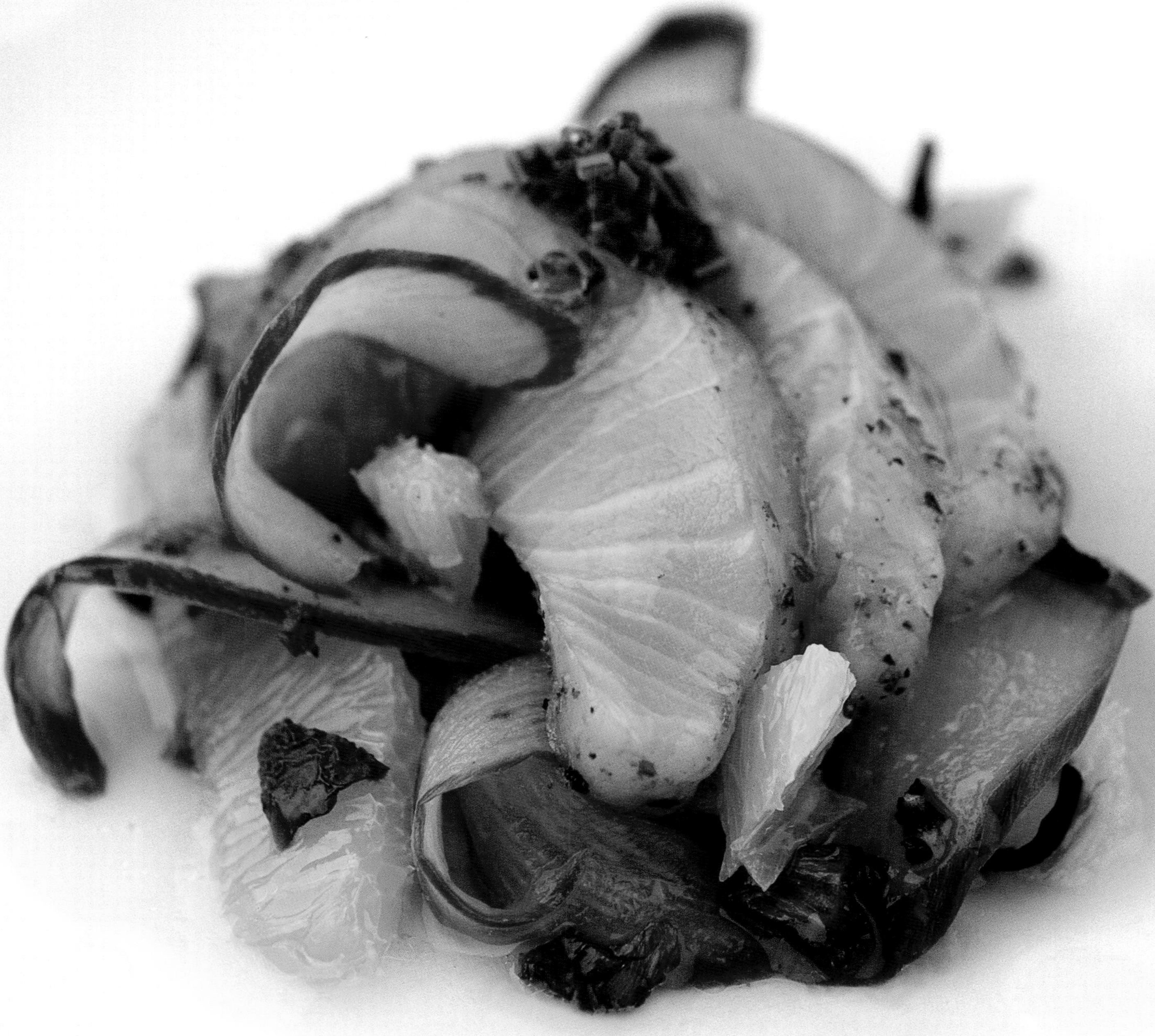

vegetable
dishes

squash with nut-brown butter, crisp sage and crushed amaretto biscuits

The combination of squash with sage is not new, but combined with the nutty aroma of brown butter, the mouth-feel of crushed Amaretto biscuits and sweet-sour apple syrup, it is good autumn comfort food.

1 small green squash

¼ cup grapeseed oil

sea salt and freshly milled white pepper

10 sprigs thyme

3 bay leaves

200g butter

2 teaspoons lemon juice

3 cups canola oil

1 cup sage leaves, loosely packed

6 Amaretto biscuits

100ml Gusto apple syrup

sea salt and freshly milled white pepper

Serves 6

Preheat the oven to 180°C.

Cut the squash (skin on) in half with a large knife, then cut each half into neat wedges. Place squash pieces in a large bowl and toss with the oil and season with salt and pepper. Place in a large roasting dish and scatter the thyme and bay leaves over. Bake for 35 minutes or until soft right through.

To make the nut-brown butter (beurre noisette), place the butter in a frypan over a medium heat and melt. Continue to cook until it turns a golden brown. Shake the frypan occasionally to ensure even colouring.

Add the lemon juice and remove from the heat to prevent the butter turning black and bitter. The acid and nutty flavours should be in balance, so take care when adding the lemon juice. The aroma should be nutty and reminiscent of roasting hazelnuts (noisette is French for hazelnut).

Heat the oil in a heavy-based saucepan and deep-fry the sage until the leaves become crisp (approximately 2 to 3 minutes). Remove leaves carefully with a slotted spoon and drain on absorbent paper.

To serve, gently lift squash from the roasting dish and arrange on a serving plate. Discard the thyme and bay leaves.

Spoon over the nut-brown butter and crumble the Amaretto biscuits over the squash. Mix a little of the roasting oil from the squash with the apple syrup and drizzle over the squash.

Scatter over the crisp sage leaves and season.

cauliflower fritters

These are a great accompaniment to roast lamb or venison. If you make them smaller the fritters are a perfect cocktail party nibble.

½ large cauliflower

60g plain flour

2 eggs

1 tablespoon lemon juice

40g each of cheddar and Gruyère cheese, grated

½ teaspoon ground nutmeg

¼ teaspoon chilli powder

¼ teaspoon cumin seeds, roasted and crushed

1 clove garlic, peeled and crushed

salt and freshly milled white pepper

500ml vegetable oil for frying

Makes 16 fritters

Cut the cauliflower into even-sized florets, and boil in salted water until tender (approximately 5 to7 minutes). Place in an ice bath to cool instantly. Drain and pat dry with absorbent paper.

Finely chop the cooked cauliflower.

Make a batter with the flour, eggs and lemon juice, then add the cheese, nutmeg, chilli, cumin and garlic. Season to taste. Add the chopped cauliflower to the batter and leave to rest for 30 minutes.

Heat the oil in a heavy-based saucepan or deep-fryer.

Spoon the mixture into the hot vegetable oil and cook for 3 to 4 minutes until they turn a deep brown colour and the cheese is melted.

parsnip mash

800g parsnips

4 sprigs thyme

1 bay leaf

1 teaspoon salt

3 cups milk

50g butter

salt and freshly milled white
  pepper

freshly grated nutmeg

Serves 6-8

Peel and core the parsnips and cut into 3cm dice. Place into a saucepan and add the thyme, bay leaf and salt. Cover with milk.

Bring to the boil and simmer for 15 minutes until tender.

Drain through a colander or sieve, reserving 100ml of the milk. Remove and discard the thyme and bay leaf.

Place the parsnips in a bowl, add the butter and purée using a whiz stick, adding enough of the reserved milk to make a smooth mash. Season to taste.

Sprinkle with nutmeg just before serving.

vegetable dishes

caramelised belgian endive

filled with goat's cheese, with crisp almonds and dates

Although these endives appear here as a side dish, they are perfect on a crisp green salad. At Soul we serve three of these on an endive and walnut salad as a starter.

8 Belgian endives
1 cup salt

filling
250g fresh goat's cheese
¼ cup fresh white breadcrumbs
3 sprigs fresh thyme
sea salt and freshly milled white pepper

½ cup unsalted butter
petals of ½ sprig lavender
sea salt and freshly milled white pepper

1 tablespoon peanut oil
2 tablespoon slivered almonds
6 Medjool dates
1 egg white
¼ cup cornflour
peanut oil for frying

sauce
2 tablespoons honey
juice of 3 oranges
1 ½ cups golden chicken stock (recipe page 139)
3 tablespoons butter
sea salt and freshly milled black pepper

Serves 6

Remove the outside layer of leaves from the endives. Trim the bottoms and remove as much of the cores as possible.

Fill a container with salt 1 to 2cm deep. Stand endives in the salt to draw out the bitterness. Cover with a damp cloth and refrigerate for 8 to 12 hours.

To prepare the filling, fold together the goat's cheese, breadcrumbs and thyme. Season with salt and pepper.

Preheat the oven to 180°C.

Remove endives from the salt and wash under cold running water. Cut 2cm off the bottom of each endive.

Remove endive leaves and lay out on a board. Divide the filling between 12 leaves. Wrap the remaining leaves around the filling and shape to re-form 12 endives.

Soften the butter and smear it over 12 pieces of foil, each large enough to wrap around an endive. Scatter lavender petals and salt and pepper on each. Wrap the foil round the endives and bake for 15 to 20 minutes.

In a frypan, heat the peanut oil and sauté the almonds until golden. Remove almonds from pan and drain on absorbent paper.

Remove the stones from the dates and cut each date into 10 pieces. Dip dates in egg white and then into the cornflour. Place the coated dates in a sieve and shake to remove excess cornflour. Heat the peanut oil and fry the coated dates in oil until crisp (1 to 2 minutes). Drain on absorbent paper.

To make the sauce, bring the honey and orange juice to the boil and reduce to a light caramel until it reaches sauce consistency. Add the chicken stock and reduce to ¼ cup. Whisk in the butter and season to taste.

To serve, carefully remove the foil from the endives and stand them on their bases in a preheated serving dish. Glaze under the grill for 1 to 2 minutes.

Spoon the sauce over, and scatter the almonds and dates on top.

braised autumn and winter greens with olive oil, garlic and lemon

Serve this dish as temperatures start to plummet. It is filling and satisfying and can be served either as a vegetable side dish or to bolster crisp duck.
You can also add Brussels sprout leaves to the mix.

200g broccolini

150g silverbeet

150g small-leaf spinach

200g wild watercress

150g wild rocket

4 tablespoons extra virgin olive oil

10 cloves garlic, peeled and thinly shaved

juice of 2 lemons

sea salt and freshly milled black pepper

lemon wedges to garnish

Serves 6

Trim the broccolini and blanch in boiling salted water for 2 minutes. Drain and refresh in cold water. Set aside.

Place all the leaves in a colander and wash under cold running water. Allow to drain for 30 minutes.

Trim and remove stalks and any damaged leaves. Cut the silverbeet into roughly 5cm lengths. Remove the lower three-quarters of the watercress stalks and cut what is left into manageable pieces able to be picked up with a fork.

In a large frypan, heat the olive oil. Add the garlic and sauté until light golden and toasted. Add the greens: broccolini first, followed by silverbeet, spinach, watercress and finally the rocket. This way they will all be fully cooked at the same time, and each will retain its individual flavour.

Cover with a lid for 1 minute, then remove the lid and toss quickly. Squeeze the lemon juice over and season to taste. (You may need to do this in two batches, depending on the size of your frypan.)

To serve, spoon into a warmed large serving dish. Accompany with fresh lemon wedges and splash with a little extra virgin olive oil.

If you like garlic, shave an extra five cloves and toast them in 2 tablespoons of oil. Scatter over the braised greens just before they go to the table.

desserts

medjool date brûlée

This is a combination of Greg Malouf's dates and my brûlée. I prefer brûlée mix cooked out on the top of the stove to the oven-baked variety. Oven baking is easier, but the taste is not as rich.

date purée

85g sugar

85ml water

170g whole Medjool dates

85ml Kahlùa

brûlée

85g sugar

12 egg yolks

1 vanilla pod

425ml cream

6 tablespoons demerara sugar

Serves 6

To make the date purée, heat the sugar and water until the sugar is dissolved. Add the whole dates and the Kahlùa. Cover with a paper lid or cartouche to stop skin from forming. Cook gently for 15 to 20 minutes.

Cool, drain and retain the cooking liquor. Remove the date skins and stones and chop finely. Mix with a little cooking liquor and return to the saucepan.

To make the brûlée, mix the sugar and yolks. Over a boiling water bath, beat them to a thick ribbon.

Split the vanilla pod in half and scrape out the seeds. Put the cream, seeds and vanilla pod in a saucepan and bring to the boil.

Pour the boiling cream slowly onto the egg-yolk mixture, whisking constantly. Put the combined mixture in a clean bowl, and put it back over the boiling water bath. Cook to a thick consistency, beating constantly.

Place 1 heaped tablespoon of the date mixture into each of six ramekins. Strain the cream and egg mixture over the date mixture. Chill to set.

To serve, sprinkle 1 tablespoon of sugar over the top of each ramekin and caramelise with a blow torch or under a very hot grill.

bitter chocolate tart with candied whole mandarins

candied mandarins

200g sugar

400ml water

½ vanilla pod, split

4 mandarins

filling

250ml cream

125ml milk

3 egg yolks

50g castor sugar

1 tablespoon Dutch cocoa

125g bitter dark chocolate (72 per cent cocoa butter), finely chopped

sweet pastry

125g unsalted butter

125g icing sugar

pinch table salt

2 eggs

250g plain flour, sifted

15g Dutch cocoa to dust

Serves 8

To candy the mandarins, bring the sugar and water to the boil over a medium heat. Add the vanilla pod. Prick the mandarins all over with a skewer and place in the syrup. (The syrup must cover the mandarins.)

Cover with a paper lid and simmer for 3 hours. Remove the saucepan from the heat and cool the mandarins in the syrup. Store the mandarins in the syrup in a glass jar in the refrigerator for up to 1 month.

For the filling, heat the cream and milk. Whisk together the egg yolks, sugar and cocoa. Remove cream and milk from heat and whisk into the egg yolk mix. Add the chocolate and stir until smooth. Set aside.

Prepare the tart case by creaming together the butter, icing sugar and salt. Whisk the eggs and pour into the butter and sugar mixture, a little at a time. Beat with a wooden spoon to combine.

Fold in sifted flour. Knead the mixture and form into a paving-stone shape. Wrap the pastry in cling film and leave to rest in the refrigerator for at least 1 hour.

Preheat the oven to 150°C. Roll out the pastry to 3mm thick on a lightly floured surface. Line a 24cm flan ring with the pastry. Prick all over with a fork to prevent the pastry from rising.

Line the pastry with baking parchment and fill with baking beans. Blind bake for 12 to 15 minutes.

Carefully lift out the paper and baking beans. Place the tart shell back in the oven and cook for a further 5 to 8 minutes until the pastry is a sandy, golden colour. Remove the shell from the oven.

Reduce the oven heat to 130°C. Pour the filling into the hot tart case and bake for 50 minutes until the filling is set.

Remove from the oven and allow to cool at room temperature for 1 hour, then place in the refrigerator to chill for 2 hours. The tart will continue to set as it cools.

To serve, cut the tart into eight wedges with a hot, sharp knife. Dust with a little Dutch cocoa. Place a wedge in the middle of each plate.

Lift mandarins from the syrup and drain. Cut each mandarin into four and arrange pieces next to the chocolate tart.

baked figs

with frangipane and raspberry sauce

This is a dish from L'Escargot in London, where I worked in the pastry section. Figs of a high-enough quality to reproduce this dish have only been available in New Zealand in the last couple of years.
The frangipane needs to be made a day in advance so it is firm enough to roll into a ball to pop into the fig.

frangipane

250g butter

250g castor sugar

5 eggs, lightly beaten

250g ground almonds

75g plain flour

raspberry sauce

125g sugar

60ml water (or enough to wet sugar)

250g raspberries, fresh or free-flow frozen

juice of ½ lemon

18–24 figs (3 or 4 per person) depending on size of figs

icing sugar to dust

Serves 6

To make the frangipane, cream the butter and sugar until pale. Slowly add half the beaten egg mixture, the dry ingredients, then the remainder of the eggs. Beat together. Place in the fridge for 24 hours.

To make the raspberry sauce, place the sugared water in a heavy-bottomed saucepan and bring to soft-ball stage (approximately 5 to 6 minutes). Add the raspberries and bring to the boil. Purée with a whiz stick and pass through a sieve. Add the lemon juice.

Preheat the oven to 220°C.

Cut a diagonal slit in each fig. Roll the frangipane into small balls, approximately 2 to 3cm in diameter (the same size as the fig). Open the slit in each fig and push in the frangipane.

Place the figs on a baking sheet and bake for 10 to 15 minutes until the frangipane has browned and the figs are soft.

Sometimes the frangipane will fall out but don't worry; in this case flavours are more important than looks!

To serve, pour the raspberry sauce onto a large platter. Carefully arrange figs on top. They can be dusted with icing sugar if the figs need additional sweetness.

baked meyer lemOn cream lime milk gelato and tropical salad

meyer lemon cream

11 free-range eggs

300g castor sugar

juice and zest of 4 Meyer lemons

400ml cream

sweet pastry

125g unsalted butter

125g icing sugar

pinch table salt

2 eggs

250g plain flour, sifted

100g icing sugar to caramelise top of lemon cream

lime milk gelato

250g castor sugar

250ml water

250ml fresh lime juice and zest of 2 limes

250ml milk

tropical salad

¼ small honeydew melon

1 mango

¼ ripe pineapple

small wedge watermelon

2 passionfruit (optional)

1 pomegranate

4 sprigs mint, chopped

Serves 6

To make the lemon cream, whisk together the eggs and sugar in a large bowl. Add the juice and zest. Add the cream and whisk to combine. Cover and place in the refrigerator to allow the lemon flavour to develop. (This is best completed one day in advance.)

To prepare the pastry base, cream together the butter, icing sugar and salt. Whisk the eggs and pour into the butter and sugar mixture, a little at a time. Beat with a wooden spoon to combine.

Fold in the flour. Knead the mixture and form into a paving-stone shape. Wrap the pastry in cling film and leave to rest in the refrigerator for at least 1 hour.

Preheat the oven to 150°C.

On a lightly floured surface, roll out the chilled pastry to 0.5cm thickness. Cut out a circle 24cm in diameter. Place on a floured baking tray and prick all over with a fork to prevent the pastry from rising.

Bake for 10 to 12 minutes until a light golden, sandy colour. Remove from the oven and allow to cool.

Turn the oven down to 120°C. Place a flan ring on a baking sheet and line with baking parchment to 1cm above the edge of the ring.

Sieve the chilled lemon filling to remove the zest, and pour filling into the lined flan ring. Remove any froth from the top of the filling. Bake for approximately 1 hour, until it is jelly-like to the touch. Remove from the oven and allow to cool for at least 2 hours.

To make the lime milk gelato, place the castor sugar and water in a saucepan and simmer until the sugar is dissolved. Add the lime juice and zest and allow mixture to cool. Add the milk, and whisk to combine.

Pour into an ice-cream maker and process, according to the maker's instructions, until the gelato holds its shape. Place in the freezer until required in a chilled, covered, stainless-steel bowl.

For the tropical salad, peel, deseed and chop the fruit, except the passionfruit, into neat 1cm dice. Cut the passionfruit in half (if using) and squeeze the pulp over the rest of the fruit. Mix all the diced fruit together.

To serve, remove the lemon cream from the flan ring by placing the pastry disc on top and inverting the baked cream onto the pastry. Dust the top with icing sugar and caramelise with a blow torch.

Place the lemon cream in the middle of a serving plate. Spoon the tropical salad around it and garnish with mint. Scoop out portions of the lime milk gelato and arrange neatly on top of the lemon cream.

chocolate mousse cake

Chocolate mousse is always the most popular dessert on the menu. Even when we have two chocolate desserts on offer, the mousse or mousse cake will always be most popular.

This recipe is a winner. The chocolate sponge can be made on a baking tray and rolled like a sponge roll when cool. Fill with strawberries and cream for a family dessert.

chocolate sponge

175g dark chocolate

6 eggs, separated

125g castor sugar

3 tablespoons strong coffee

dark chocolate mousse

250g dark chocolate

120g unsalted butter, cubed

4 eggs, separated

60ml cream, lightly whipped

1 tablespoon castor sugar

15g Dutch cocoa to dust

Serves 6-8

Preheat the oven to 190°C. Line an 8-inch round spring cake tin with buttered greaseproof paper.

To make the sponge, melt the chocolate over a double boiler. Set aside to cool.

In a mixer with a whisk attachment, cream the egg yolks and castor sugar until pale and creamy. Fold in the cooled, melted chocolate and the coffee.

Whisk the egg whites to soft peaks and fold carefully into the chocolate mixture, a quarter of the whites at a time.

Pour mixture into the cake tin and bake for 10 to 15 minutes until the sponge bounces back when softly pressed. Set aside to cool.

To make the mousse, melt the chocolate over a double boiler. Remove from heat and whisk until smooth.

Add the butter and whisk until incorporated. Add the egg yolks and whisk. Gently fold in the cream and set aside.

Whisk the eggs whites, adding the sugar slowly until soft peaks form. Fold gently into the chocolate mix, a quarter at a time.

Cut the cooled sponge into two rounds, horizontally. Line the cake tin with baking paper and place one round of sponge at the bottom of the tin. Pour in the mousse and cover with the other round.

Refrigerate for 2 hours, then dust with cocoa powder before serving.

With a hot knife cut into six or eight portions and place each portion on a plate. Serve with fresh raspberries or strawberries and a dollop of whipped cream.

feijOa beignets on lime and ginger frozen parfait

lime and ginger parfait

125g water

100g sugar

5 eggs

500ml cream, whipped

80g caramelised ginger
   (recipe page 94)

zest of 3 limes

1 portion beer batter
   (recipe page 28) without
   seasoning

1.5 litres peanut oil for deep
   frying

2 large feijoas per person

cinnamon sugar

1 teaspoon ground cinnamon

2 teaspoons castor sugar

Serves 6

Grease a terrine mould and line with cling film.

To make the parfait, combine the water and sugar in a saucepan and heat, stirring continuously, until the sugar is dissolved. Bring the sugar syrup to the boil.

Whisk the eggs with an electric mixer. With the mixer on full, slowly pour the boiling syrup into the eggs and whisk until cool.

Fold in the whipped cream, caramelised ginger and lime zest. Pour into the lined mould, cover with cling film and freeze overnight.

Prepare the beer batter according to method on page 28 without seasoning.

To make the beignets, pour the peanut oil into a heavy-based saucepan and heat to 160°C, or use a domestic deep-fryer.

Cut the feijoas in half and scoop out the flesh. Dip the flesh into the beer batter and deep-fry until golden brown and crispy, making sure not to overload the pan. Drain on absorbent paper.

Mix the cinnamon and castor sugar together for dusting.

To serve, slice the parfait into 1cm-thick slices and place on plates. Arrange several beignets on top, and dust with cinnamon sugar.

french peach tart with caramel sauce

A variation on the classic French apple tart, this can be made with apples if stone fruit is out of season.

caramel sauce

250g castor sugar

¼ cup water

375ml cream

almond sponge (frangipane)

100g unsalted butter

100g castor sugar

2 eggs, room temperature

100g ground almonds

25g plain flour

1 pkt frozen all butter puff pastry

6 ripe peaches

½ cup apricot jam

3 tablespoons water

Serves 6

To make the sauce, cook the sugar and water in a heavy-based saucepan over a medium heat until deep brown and well caramelised (approximately 15 minutes). Remove from heat and carefully pour in the cream. Stir gently.

Return to a medium heat and simmer for 4–5 minutes. Remove from heat. Set aside until required.

To make the almond sponge, cream the butter and sugar until pale. Add one of the eggs and whisk well. Add the ground almonds and flour, then the second egg. Refrigerate.

Roll out the puff pastry to 3mm thick and cut out six 15cm-diameter circles. Refrigerate on a baking paper-lined baking sheet. (If the baking sheet doesn't fit in the fridge, layer the pastry circles with greaseproof paper between each and refrigerate. These can be cut out the night before and covered with cling film.)

Preheat oven to 180°C.

To prepare the tarts, peel, halve and stone the peaches. Slice into even, 5mm-thick wedges.

Place 1 tablespoon of almond sponge in the centre of each pastry circle. Arrange the slices of peach in a flan style, leaving 1cm of bare pastry around the outside edge. Bake for 15 to 20 minutes until golden brown.

Mix the jam and water and microwave for 1 minute on high power. Sieve to remove any lumps or skin. Glaze the tarts with the jam using a pastry brush while they are still hot.

To serve, microwave the caramel sauce for 1 minute on high power.

Spoon the caramel sauce onto each of six large plates to form a pool slightly larger than the tarts. Place each tart onto a pool of sauce. Serve with vanilla ice-cream.

lime-curd tartlets with caramelised ginger

Limes can vary greatly in size and the amount of juice they yield. We used juicy limes that weighed about 50g each.

caramelised ginger

1 cup castor sugar

1 cup water

125g root ginger, peeled and julienned

sweet pastry

450g flour

340g butter

170g castor sugar

4 whole egg yolks

zest of 2 lemons

lime curd

3 large eggs

340g castor sugar

150g unsalted butter, cubed

zest of 4 limes

juice of 9 limes

icing sugar to dust

Makes 12 tartlets

Preheat the oven to 90ºC.

Combine the sugar and water in a saucepan and place over a medium heat until the sugar is dissolved. Set aside while you make the caramelised ginger. Bring a saucepan of water to the boil. Add the ginger and simmer for 1 minute. Repeat four times, using fresh water each time.

Place the sugar syrup into a saucepan, add the ginger and bring to the boil. Reduce the heat and simmer until the ginger is translucent.

Drain the ginger and spread out evenly on a baking try lined with greaseproof paper. Bake in the oven for 1 hour until crunchy but not coloured. Set aside to cool.

To make the pastry, use the paddle of an electric beater to rub the flour and butter together until the mixture resembles breadcrumbs. Add the sugar and then the yolks with the lemon zest. Do not overwork the pastry as it will toughen and shrink during baking.

Lightly grease a set of tartlet tins and dust lightly with flour.

Roll out the pastry on a lightly floured surface until 3mm thick. Using a pastry cutter slightly bigger than the tartlet tins, cut out 12 rounds.

Place the pastry rounds into the tins and trim the edges with a small, sharp knife. Place in the refrigerator for approximately 20 minutes.

Blind bake the cases for approximately 15 minutes or until lightly coloured. Remove from the oven and cool on a baking tray.

To make the curd, whisk the eggs and sugar in a large, heat-proof bowl until well combined but not frothy. Add the butter, zest and juice and stir with a wooden spoon over a saucepan of simmering water for approximately 20 minutes until the mixture thickens and coats the back of the spoon. Remove from heat and allow to cool.

The curd can also be made in a saucepan. Cook the curd in a heavy-based saucepan at simmering point over a medium-high heat for approximately 5 minutes. As soon as bubbles appear, remove from heat, still stirring, and allow to cool. To serve, spoon the cooled curd into the pastry cases. Top with the caramelised ginger and dust with icing sugar.

soul bar & bistro

guest
chefs

bill marchetti
melbourne

I have known Bill since 1993 when I went to Melbourne to learn how to make pasta the Italian way. At that point there was a shift in New Zealand cuisine taste towards Mediterranean/Italian food. As New Zealand has not had the benefits of Italian migration (unlike Australia), there was a dearth of learning models in New Zealand.

I had heard that Bill's restaurant, The Latin in Melbourne, was one of the best and I managed to talk my way into obtaining work experience (without pay) in his kitchen after meeting his wife at a social occasion. Bill was, probably fortunately, overseas. I believe that I was the first woman to ever have entered his kitchen in a working capacity and, on his return, he demanded to know how this woman (me) managed to be there with lipstick and nail polish. Fortunately the head chef backed me up and I was allowed to continue my education.

Not long after that, I invited Bill to be a guest chef at Ramses. Between us, we reproduced his whole menu from The Latin and it provided such a different taste sensation in New Zealand that those who were there still talk about the experience. The procurement of the product for that menu in 1993 was a logistical nightmare. A number of the ingredients needed to be imported. However, it was pleasing that several New Zealand producers went to amazing lengths to source, develop and grow some of the essential items needed. Experiences like these have been beneficial to New Zealand cuisine in that they have helped develop new and diverse product choice and selection.

Bill has been a guest chef for me on four occasions. Each time has been an unqualified success. For my part, I continue to be inspired by his food quality and passion.

Sadly The Latin is no more, and Bill is presently in India on yet another cuisine adventure. He is now sending me trained chefs from New Delhi.

Bill's recipes, which I have chosen for inclusion, form the basis for dishes that have appeared regularly on my menus over the last decade.

crayfish and whisky risotto

1 whole crayfish, approximately 1kg

1.5 litres fish stock (recipe page 138)

1 cup finely diced onion

50g butter

50ml light olive oil

500g arborio rice

100ml dry white wine

100ml whisky

sea salt and freshly milled black pepper

100ml whisky, extra

100ml cream

grated parmesan to serve

Serves 4 as a main or 8 as an entrée

This great dish, with very unusual flavours, is still requested more than 10 years after it first appeared at Ramses during Bill's guest chef visit in 1993. Expensive and very rich, a small portion will suffice.

If the crayfish is alive, kill it by placing it in the freezer for a couple of hours.

Boil the crayfish in ample salted water for about 8 minutes.

When cool enough to handle, remove all the meat from the head and tail and cut into 1cm dice. Be careful to retain the 'mustard' (the brown juices) and any roe from the crayfish head — this will greatly improve the flavour of the risotto.

Heat the fish stock to boiling. Sauté the onion in the butter and olive oil until translucent. Add the rice and sauté for a couple of minutes to seal. Deglaze with the white wine and the first measure of whisky. Cook and stir rice until the whisky is absorbed. Season with salt and pepper.

Add the hot stock ladle by ladle, stirring continuously, adding another ladle only when the previous one has been absorbed. When the rice is almost cooked (approximately 20 minutes), add the crayfish and mustard, the second measure of whisky and the cream. Allow to simmer for another couple of minutes until the cream has reduced slightly to a light coating consistency.

Spoon onto plates.

Taste and adjust the seasoning.

Serve with grated parmesan.

potato gnocchi

with pork, veal and tomato ragoût

I tasted this dish in 1993, on my first visit to The Latin. The amazingly rich sauce is well worth the preparation time. All the meat is hand-cut, not minced. A barrister friend of mine helped me out with a small court case and, in lieu of payment, I solemnly promised never to take this dish off the menu. He is still a regular visitor to Soul, and nine times out of ten he orders this dish.

2 pig's trotters

100ml extra virgin olive oil

75g butter

200g prosciutto fat

250g peeled and diced onion

1 teaspoon chopped garlic

1 small hot chilli, seeded and sliced

150g diced carrot

150g diced celery

1kg (nett) veal blade, trimmed, sinews removed and cut into 5mm dice

750g (nett) pork shoulder, trimmed, sinews removed and cut into 5mm dice

20ml dry white wine

650ml meat stock (recipe page 139)

1 orange, peeled and halved

1 bouquet garni, wrapped and tied in cheesecloth, consisting of:

2 bay leaves
4 juniper berries
4 cloves
half a cinnamon stick
4 branches fresh oregano

500g peeled, seeded and diced tomatoes

200g tomato paste

20g dried porcini mushrooms, soaked in warm water to reconstitute

salt and freshly milled black pepper

½ cup chopped basil

150g cooked gnocchi per person (recipe page 137)

Serves 20

Boil the pig's trotters for about 45 minutes. Refresh them (i.e. run under cold water until cool) and discard the cooking liquid.

In a large braising saucepan, heat the oil and butter. Add the prosciutto fat and sauté until it begins to brown. Add the onion, garlic and chilli and sauté until the onion is translucent.

Add the carrot and celery and sauté until soft. Add the meat and sauté until it is lightly coloured (approximately 15 minutes).

Deglaze with the wine and reduce for about 10 minutes. Add the meat stock, orange halves, boiled pig's trotters and bouquet garni. Add the tomatoes, tomato paste and mushrooms including liquid that the mushrooms have been reconstituted in, and season with salt and pepper.

Cook for about 40 minutes. Remove and discard the pig's trotters and bouquet garni. When the sauce is cooked and cooled, add the chopped basil.

To serve, bring a saucepan of salted water to the boil, then add the cooked gnocchi. As they rise to the top, remove them with a slotted spoon and toss them in some of the warmed ragoût.

bill marchetti

tira mi su

'pick me up'

This dish was on the Corbans Wine and Food Challenge menu when we won in 1993. It was paired with a glass of tawny port: the perfect match, as the spice in the port was a great foil for the richness of the dessert.

We always make it in large bowls. The waiter brings the whole bowl to the table and then proceeds to portion the tira mi su for the guests.

200ml double-strong espresso coffee

50ml Strega liqueur

100ml dry Italian marsala

1 cup castor sugar

3 whole eggs

50ml brandy

400g mascarpone

500g sponge cake

200g bitter chocolate, chopped

1 tablespoon dark cocoa powder for dusting

Serves 8-10

In a bowl, combine the coffee, Strega, half the marsala and half the sugar. Set aside.

In a copper or stainless-steel bowl combine the eggs, brandy, and the rest of the sugar and marsala.

Half-fill a low-sided braising pan with water and bring it to the boil. Reduce to a simmer. Start whisking the egg mixture off the heat until it starts to fluff up. Place the bowl a few centimetres above the simmering water and keep whisking energetically. As the eggs begin to aerate, lower the bowl into the water. Keep whisking until stiff ribbons of egg sabayon form, then whisk the mixture over ice until cool.

Gradually whisk in the mascarpone, a little at a time. The mixture should now have the appearance of soft whipped cream.

To assemble the tira mi su, cut the sponge into three layers. Lay it out on a tray and soak with the coffee and liqueur mix.

Place a layer of sponge in the bottom of a large serving bowl, topped with one-third of the sabayon. Sprinkle with half the chopped chocolate and add another layer of sponge. Top with sabayon, chocolate and sponge, finishing with sabayon.

Sprinkle the cocoa liberally on top. Leave to set in the fridge for at least 3 hours before serving.

bill marchetti

greg malouf
melbourne

Greg Malouf has inspired a generation of young chefs and transformed the Melbourne restaurant scene with his passion for the flavours of North Africa and the Middle East. Born in Melbourne, to Lebanese parents, he served his formal apprenticeship in several of Melbourne's finest restaurants before working in France, Italy, Austria and Hong Kong.

Drawing on his cultural heritage and European training, Greg has created a unique style of cooking that combines Middle Eastern tradition with contemporary flair. He is the co-author of three cookery books — *Arabesque*, *Moorish* and *Saha* — and is resident chef at Momo's, in Melbourne.

My first introduction to Greg did not go quite as I planned. I met him in Auckland, after he had done a brief stint at Huka Lodge, to encourage him to be a guest chef at Soul. In order to check my credentials, he asked me several oblique cooking questions. I had no answer to 'How many pin bones are there in a salmon?', and I am still unsure whether there is an answer to this.

Obviously I passed his test, however, and we have now become good friends. When I moved to Soul, I was keen to introduce a new style of cooking to the Auckland public. He provided inspirational assistance with a number of dishes, many of which are still on the menu. I believe that Soul retains a modern Middle Eastern twist; the entrées predominantly feature these flavours.

Greg continues to maintain an association with Soul, and he and I are in regular contact over trends in food. I am delighted that he has offered to contribute these recipes to this book. He has cooked these dishes at a guest night at Soul and they were splendidly received.

salmon kibbeh nayeh

300g Akaroa salmon, finely minced and chilled

2 purple shallots, peeled and finely chopped

⅓ cup white fine-grade burghul, soaked for 8 minutes in ½ cup water, then squeezed dry

⅓ teaspoon allspice

freshly milled white pepper

2 very small chillies, seeded, scraped and finely chopped

1 teaspoon sea salt

120ml extra virgin olive oil

⅓ cup coriander leaves

⅓ cup mint leaves

⅓ cup flat parsley leaves

2 pickled artichokes, sliced

1 small red onion, peeled and finely sliced

juice of ½ lemon

sea salt and freshly milled white pepper

Serves 6 as a starter

To make the kibbeh, chill a stainless-steel or glass bowl. In it mix the salmon, shallots, burghul, allspice, pepper, chilli and salt with one-third of the olive oil.

In another bowl, mix the herb leaves and sliced artichokes with the onion, lemon, one-third of the olive oil, and salt and pepper to taste.

To serve, spoon the kibbeh onto a flat dish and spread with a spatula to an even thickness. Place a small mound of salad on top. Drizzle the remaining olive oil around the salmon.

Scoop up with flat Lebanese bread (available at good delis and supermarkets).

musakhan 'she has fever'
chicken baked in mountain bread with spinach and chickpea stew

This recipe is based on a Bedouin dish, where chicken is cooked on bread with lots of sumac and bitter wild greens. Eat the juice-soaked bread with the chicken — definitely get your hands dirty — Greg Malouf

spinach and chickpea stew

40ml olive oil

2 onions, peeled and finely grated

2 cloves garlic, peeled and finely chopped

1 teaspoon ground cinnamon

1 teaspoon ground nutmeg

1½ teaspoons sumac

3 bunches spinach leaves, blanched, squeezed and chopped

150g cooked or tinned chickpeas

300ml chicken stock (recipe page 138), divided into two 150ml portions

juice of ½ lemon

150g toasted pine nuts, roughly crushed

6 chicken legs

2 cloves garlic, crushed with
    ½ teaspoon salt
    ½ teaspoon ground cinnamon
    ½ teaspoon ground cumin
    ½ teaspoon ground black pepper

2 tablespoons olive oil

6 large square pieces of mountain bread

olive oil

salt and pepper

Serves 6

Heat the olive oil in a large, non-stick frypan. Sauté the onions and garlic until soft and any liquid has evaporated. Add the spices and stir well.

Add the chopped spinach, then the chickpeas. Use a fork to lightly crush the chickpeas, then add half of the stock. Turn up the heat and boil for approximately 5 minutes until the stock has evaporated. Remove from the heat and add the lemon juice and pine nuts. Leave to cool, then refrigerate until needed.

Cut the chicken legs in half, separating the drumsticks from the thighs, then make a single cut inwards to expose the bones. This will help them cook more quickly.

Mix together the garlic, salt and spices and rub all over the chicken pieces. Leave in a cool place to marinate for 1 to 2 hours.

Heat the oil in a large, non-stick frypan and colour the chicken to a golden brown. Remove from the pan and keep warm.

Preheat the oven to 200ºC. Cut six pieces of baking parchment roughly 3cm larger than the squares of mountain bread. Lay the paper, one square at a time, on the work surface and place a piece of bread on top of each. Spoon a dollop of spinach in the centre of each piece of bread, and place a chicken leg (a drumstick and a thigh) on top.

Gather the pieces of paper (and bread) together above the chicken and tie with kitchen string to form a little bag. Place on a baking tray and cover with tinfoil to prevent the paper getting crispy and the string from burning. Bake for 20 minutes.

Tip the remaining spinach mix into a saucepan and add the remaining chicken stock and olive oil. Season to taste. Cook for 10 minutes over a gentle heat.

Serve an individual parcel for each person to unwrap at the table with bowls of spinach stew.

burnt hOney & yOghurt panna cotta

with honey caramel

honey caramel

100g castor sugar

100g honey

100ml water

few drops orange-blossom
   water (optional)

1 tablespoon walnut oil

panna cotta

240g honey

90ml orange juice

3 leaves gelatine

300ml cream

800g natural yoghurt

18 strawberries, hulled
   and halved

4 mandarins, peeled and
   segmented

6 tablespoons castor sugar

1 packet fairy floss, for
   garnish

Serves 8

To make the honey caramel, place the castor sugar, honey and half the water in a saucepan, and bring to the boil. Simmer until the mixture turns light brown and caramelises.

Remove from heat. Carefully add the remainder of the water and stir. A few drops of orange-blossom water can be added.

Lightly grease eight moulds or ramekins (130ml capacity) with the walnut oil.

To make the panna cotta, boil the honey for approximately 6 minutes, until it starts to darken and caramelise. Carefully add the orange juice and continue cooking until the honey is dissolved. Remove from the heat.

Soak the gelatine in a little cold water until it softens, then squeeze well and add to the honey mixture. Leave to cool slightly.

In a large bowl, stir together the cream and yoghurt. Add a

spoonful to the honey mixture and stir in well. Tip the honey mixture into the cream mixture, stirring until evenly combined.

Strain the panna cotta mixture through a fine sieve and pour into moulds. Refrigerate until set (6 to 8 hours).

Preheat the grill to its maximum temperature. Dust the strawberry and mandarin pieces with castor sugar.

Gently remove the panna cotta from each mould (running the moulds under a little hot water helps). Place each panna cotta in the centre of a plate.

Place the fruit under the hot grill until the sugar caramelises. Remove and arrange around each panna cotta. Serve with honey caramel.

Garnish with fairy floss, which can be purchased from food stores like Epicurean, Zarbo and Sabato.

charlie trotter
chicago

Soul had the privilege of being selected by *Cuisine* magazine as host restaurant for the *Cuisine* Readers' Dinner with Charlie Trotter. This was Charlie's first (and we hope not his last) visit to New Zealand. He was here as a guest of the Hospitality Standards Institute to judge the modern cookery Chef Apprentice of the Year award and to speak at the institute's conference.

Charlie Trotter began his career as a professional chef in 1982, and has since travelled and worked all over the world. In 1987 he opened the now world-famous Charlie Trotter's in Chicago, Illinois. For more than 16 years it has been regarded as one of the finest restaurants in the world, winning many international awards. Charlie is the author of nine cookbooks and is the host of an award-winning television series. He is also a dedicated philanthropist and a huge supporter of education in the culinary arts.

His visit to Soul was an immediate sell-out. Some of those attending were quite bemused when he stated in his speech that in his view, 'the customer is not always right'. I had always believed the opposite — at least until then.

The Soul kitchen brigade was once again challenged by the task of finding and testing alternative ingredients for those found in Chicago but not in New Zealand. And we did it successfully enough to receive Charlie's praise.

Charlie's presence in the restaurant and the manner in which he addressed all kitchen personnel provided encouragement and inspiration.

For this book, Charlie has chosen three dishes, one from each of three of his books. They have been slightly adapted to suit New Zealand product availability.

hapuku with pinot noir-stewed shallots and veal stock reduction

This dish was served as a starter at Soul. If you were to cook it for a main course, allow 200g fresh fish per person. Delicious with a pinot noir.

1½ shallots, peeled and thinly sliced

3 cups pinot noir

16 baby carrots, washed

2 tablespoons extra virgin olive oil

4 medium shiitake mushrooms

2 cloves garlic, peeled

5 sprigs thyme

1 cup mushroom stock (recipe page 140)

sea salt and freshly milled black pepper

1 cup veal stock reduction (recipe page 140)

1 tablespoon hoisin sauce

3 teaspoons tamari (soya sauce with no wheat)

2 teaspoons rice wine vinegar

4 fillets hapuku, each approximately 100g

sea salt and freshly milled black pepper

2 teaspoons grapeseed oil

Serves 4

Preheat oven to 180°C.

Place the shallots and pinot noir in a small saucepan. Simmer over medium heat for 20 to 30 minutes, or until all the wine has been absorbed into the shallots.

In an ovenproof dish, place the carrots and 1 tablespoon of olive oil. Roast in oven, turning occasionally, for 15 to 20 minutes or until tender.

Trim the stems off the mushrooms and rinse. Place in an ovenproof dish with the garlic, thyme, mushroom stock, and remaining 1 tablespoon of olive oil. Season to taste and cover with tinfoil. Roast for 30 minutes at 180°C, or until the mushrooms are just cooked.

Place the veal stock reduction, hoisin, tamari, and rice wine vinegar in a medium saucepan and bring to a simmer.

Season both sides of the hapuku. Sauté in a very hot pan in the grapeseed oil for 2 minutes each side.

To serve, place some of the shallots in the centre of each plate and top with a piece of fish. Arrange the roasted carrots and shiitake mushrooms around the hapuku and spoon the veal stock reduction around the plate.

lamb rack

with cumin-scented mushrooms, golden raisins, and potato purée

This lamb dish originally had fresh porcini mushrooms, which, alas, are not available in New Zealand. The field mushrooms do work but if you feel the need, add 10g of reconstituted dried porcini for extra intensity. The raisins provide a delicious sweetness to complement the lamb. When the spring lambs arrive, they can be very small. If so, you may need to serve 1 whole rack per person.

oregano oil
½ cup firmly packed fresh oregano leaves

1 cup firmly packed spinach leaves

½ cup plus 1 tablespoon grapeseed oil

¼ cup olive oil

potato purée
1kg Agria potatoes, peeled and quartered

½ cup milk

2 tablespoons unsalted butter

sea salt and freshly milled black pepper

cumin-scented mushrooms
2 cups sliced field mushrooms

1 ½ tablespoons butter

1 teaspoon coarsely ground cumin seeds

1 tablespoon rice vinegar

⅓ cup water

1 tablespoon olive oil

½ cup golden raisins

sea salt and freshly milled black pepper

2 lamb racks with 4 chops each, frenched

sea salt and freshly milled black pepper

2 teaspoons coarsely ground cumin seeds

1 ½ tablespoons grapeseed oil

4 teaspoons small fresh oregano leaves

freshly milled black pepper

Serves 4

To prepare the oregano oil, in a small sauté pan over medium heat sauté the oregano leaves and spinach with 1 tablespoon of grapeseed oil for 2 minutes, or until the spinach is wilted. Immediately refresh in iced water and drain.

Coarsely chop the mixture and squeeze out the excess water. Purée the spinach mixture with the remaining ½ cup grapeseed oil and the olive oil for 3 to 4 minutes, or until bright green. Pour into a container, cover, and refrigerate for 1 day.

Strain the oil through a fine-mesh sieve and discard the solids. Refrigerate for 1 day, decant, and refrigerate until ready to use (for up to 2 weeks).

To prepare the potato purée, place the potatoes in a saucepan filled with boiling water. Cook until tender, 20 minutes approximately. Strain the water off the potatoes. Add the milk and butter to the potato pan and return to heat. Bring back to the boil. Remove from heat and mash until smooth. Season and keep warm.

To prepare the mushrooms, place in a sauté pan with the butter and cumin. Sauté over medium heat for 2 minutes. Add the rice vinegar, water, olive oil, and raisins and cook for 3 minutes, or until the mushrooms are tender. Season to taste.

Preheat the oven to 200°C.

To prepare the lamb, season and sprinkle with cumin. Place in a hot roasting pan with the oil and sear over medium-high heat for 3 minutes on each side. Roast in the oven for 15 minutes, or until cooked medium-rare.

Rest for 3 minutes and slice into chops.

To serve, spoon a large ring of warm potato purée onto each plate. Spoon the mushroom mixture and any juices that remain in the pan into the centre of the ring. Place two lamb chops over the mushrooms and drizzle the oregano oil around the plate. Sprinkle with oregano leaves and pepper.

charlie trotter

warm apple tart

with date ice-cream and red-wine caramel sauce

Everyone loves a good apple tart and this one is exceptional. At Soul we have used the red-wine caramel sauce on other desserts.

date ice-cream

400g dried dates, pitted and chopped

1 vanilla pod, split lengthwise with the pulp scraped out and reserved

2¼ cups cream

¾ cup milk

6 egg yolks

red-wine caramel sauce

1 cup pinot noir

1½ cups sugar

4 tablespoons butter

1 vanilla pod, split lengthwise with the pulp scraped out and reserved

½ portion short pastry (recipe page 136)

5 tablespoons chopped pecans

3 Granny Smith apples, peeled and cut into 20 thick wedges

Serves 4

To make the ice-cream, place the dates, vanilla pod pulp, cream and milk in a medium-size saucepan. Bring to a simmer over medium heat.

Place the egg yolks in a medium-size bowl and whisk until smooth. Slowly pour the cream mixture into the yolks, continually whisking.

Place mixture in a blender and purée until smooth. Return to the saucepan and cook for 3 minutes, continuously stirring. Pass through a fine-mesh sieve, then cool. Freeze in an ice-cream machine, and keep frozen until ready to use.

To make the sauce, place the wine in a small saucepan and simmer for 20 minutes, or until reduced to quarter of a cup.

Place the sugar in a medium-size heavy-based saucepan. Gently melt the sugar over medium-low heat until golden brown and caramelised. Add the butter and vanilla pulp and cook for 2 minutes. Add the apple wedges and cook for 5 to 7 minutes, or until the apples are half cooked. Remove the apples from the caramel and reserve both separately.

Preheat the oven to 180°C.

Roll out the pastry to 30mm thick and line four ring or tart moulds approximately 7cm by 1.5cm. Place the moulds on a parchment-lined baking-sheet. Line the bottom of each mould with ½ teaspoon of the chopped pecans. Place 4 to 5 apple wedges in each tart and brush with some of the caramel sauce.

Add the remaining caramel sauce to the red-wine reduction and whisk until smooth. Fold in the remaining pecans and keep warm.

Bake the tarts for 15 to 20 minutes, or until golden brown. Remove from the moulds and serve immediately.

To serve, place an apple tart in the centre of each plate. Spoon the red-wine caramel sauce around the tart and place a scoop of the date ice-cream at the side of the tart.

geeling

As everyone who has visited Soul will know, Geeling is a star of the restaurant. She has worked with me on and off for more than 10 years, starting at Ramses as restaurant manager.

Many people will also know Gee from her acting roles. David Bowie's 'China Girl' is possibly best known for her performances as Jasmine Sage in the television show *Gloss* in the 1980s, and she is also known as a radio hostess.

With this background in the media and in restaurant management, it was only natural that she should be chosen to host the cooking segments of *Asia Down Under*, which has been on our television screens for the last few years. The following recipes have all been cooked by her on this show.

It is wonderful that Gee has this opportunity to showcase yet another of her many attributes. The kitchen staff at Soul were all extremely excited by her presence in the kitchen, preparing these dishes for photography.

Geeling is the operations manager at Soul, responsible for the management of the 'chaos' on the restaurant floor. She selects, manages and trains approximately 60 to 70 staff. This year Soul was awarded the *Cuisine* Restaurant of the Year Service Award which was a well-earned plaudit not only for Geeling but also for the rest of the management team.

Vietnamese pancakes
(banh xeo)

chilli sauce

1 clove garlic, peeled

2 red chillies (the smaller, the hotter!)

2 teaspoons white sugar

juice of 1 lemon

2–3 tablespoons fish sauce

water to thin

filling

500g minced pork

1 small onion, peeled and chopped

soya sauce to taste

2 cups mung bean sprouts

500g cooked shrimp, peeled (defrosted)

pancake batter

1 ¾ cups rice flour

2 cups coconut milk

1 egg

1 tablespoon turmeric

2 spring onions, thinly sliced

fish sauce to taste

vegetable oil to fry

1 iceberg lettuce separated into leaf 'cups'

fresh mint or basil to taste

Serves about 10 pancakes depending on the size of your pan

To make the dipping sauce, grind the garlic and chilli, using a mortar and pestle, until well blended. Put the rest of the ingredients into a bowl, add garlic and chilli mixture and stir well until sugar is dissolved.

To make the pancake filling, stir-fry the pork with the onion and soya sauce until well cooked. Add the bean sprouts and stir-fry until slightly softened. Add the shrimp and stir-fry until warmed through.

To make the pancake batter, mix all the ingredients together until there are no lumps. The batter mix should be quite runny.

Into a non-stick frypan or wok heat a little oil, then pour in enough batter to make a thin pancake. Once the bottom of the pancake is cooked (2–3 minutes), turn it over. Slide onto a tray and keep warm.

Serve the filling in the lettuce cups with a pile of folded pancakes on one side and a side dish of chilli sauce. The traditional way of serving this dish is with the filling in the pancakes and the pancakes tucked into the lettuce cups. Add some fresh herbs if desired. Dip into or drizzle chilli sauce over.

Anthony Archer is our IT consultant at Soul. He's not only good with computers, he's also a great cook, and devilishly handsome. When he appeared on the show, we were inundated with requests from female viewers who wanted him to do another segment with us! And I thought they were just watching for the cooking — Geeling

grilled five-spice chicken

This is the perfect summer barbecue recipe. I know this by the way it disappeared so quickly once we had finished the shoot! Even our sound guy Elton (who thinks that Kentucky Fried Chicken is exotic) liked this one, and that's saying something — Geeling

soy-lime dipping sauce

½ clove garlic, peeled

1 whole fresh bird's-eye chilli (hot)

1 tablespoon white sugar

¼ cup dark soya sauce

juice and pulp of 2 fresh limes (approximately 2 tablespoons)

water to taste

five-spice chicken

1 whole chicken, preferably free-range, rinsed and dried

3 tablespoons vegetable oil

2 tablespoons dark soya sauce

3 tablespoons minced ginger

2 tablespoons minced garlic

2 tablespoons white sugar

2 teaspoons ground turmeric

1 teaspoon Chinese five-spice powder

½ tablespoon salt

4 whole star anise, lightly toasted in a dry pan for 3 minutes, then pounded or ground into a fine powder

Serves 4

To make the dipping sauce, place the garlic, chilli and sugar in a mortar and pound into a paste. Transfer to a small bowl and add the soya sauce, lime juice and pulp and water. Stir until well blended. (This sauce will keep up to 3 weeks if stored in the refrigerator in an air-tight jar.)

Cut the chicken into six pieces (for faster cooking, make one or two slashes in each piece). In a bowl, combine the oil, soya sauce, ginger, garlic, sugar, turmeric, five-spice powder and salt. Stir well to blend. Add the chicken pieces and turn several times to coat them evenly. Marinate in the refrigerator for at least 4 hours.

Heat your grill or barbecue. Thirty minutes before cooking, add the freshly toasted star anise powder to the marinated chicken, turning so the meat is coated evenly.

Place the chicken, skin-side up, on the grill. Cook for 10 minutes, then turn over and grill until the chicken is cooked and the juices run clear (approximately another 10 minutes, depending on the thickness). While grilling, move the chicken pieces around so that they cook evenly.

Transfer the chicken to a serving platter and serve with the dipping sauce.

balinese duck (bebek betutu)

4 duck legs

paste

peanut cooking oil

6 shallots, peeled and halved

2 cloves garlic, peeled and halved

6 candlenuts

5cm piece root ginger, sliced

7.5–10cm piece fresh turmeric, sliced

1 tablespoon galangal powder

1 tablespoon whole black peppercorns

6 whole bird's-eye chillies

2 tablespoons coriander seeds

20g shrimp paste (about 1 tablespoon)

2 teaspoons salt

3 stalks lemongrass, white part only

6 kaffir lime leaves

wrapping

2 sheets banana leaves

Serves 4

Remove the thigh bones from the duck legs and trim off excess fat. Wipe legs dry and set aside.

Heat a wok or frypan. Add the oil and sauté all the paste ingredients (except lemongrass and lime leaves) until fragrant. Put the sautéed ingredients in a food processor, add the lemongrass and lime leaves and blend until a coarse paste is formed.

Soften the banana leaves by passing them over a flame or heat from the barbecue until pliable.

Rub the duck legs with the paste and wrap individually in banana leaves (if you can't find banana leaves you can use tinfoil, but it won't taste quite the same). Tie packets with string. Steam for 40 minutes in a steamer.

Once steamed, grill the wrapped duck legs on the barbecue for about 5 minutes each side.

Cut string, unwrap and serve.

This recipe came from the lovely Balinese chef at the CityLife Hotel in Auckland. When we were sourcing ingredients we couldn't find the banana leaves. Luckily the chef had a banana tree growing in his backyard, so he brought some along for us! You could also use pre-soaked and softened bamboo leaves — Geeling

philip johnson
brisbane

Philip Johnson and his restaurant e'cco Bistro in Brisbane have consistently won numerous state and national awards in Australia.

Philip has been Air New Zealand's Australian consulting chef, and has made a considerable number of guest chef appearances internationally. He has contributed recipes to a number of prominent publications, as well as being the author of three of his own cookbooks.

Philip was a Soul guest chef for two summer luncheons. I chose to display Philip's cuisine at lunchtime because his dishes have a Pacific influence suited to the outdoor environment of Soul's terrace. Not only did those attending thoroughly enjoy his cuisine, but Soul was delighted to be able to make a worthwhile donation from the ticket sales to the Breast Cancer Foundation.

Here are three of the dishes cooked by Philip at the Soul luncheons. The quail dish is a personal favourite of mine. I have no doubt you and your guests will enjoy them as well.

spirits bay scallops

in pancetta with parsnip mash and curry vinaigrette

Scallop season starts in August and runs through until March. Try not to use frozen scallops as they have water in them and it's hard to get them to colour well.

curry vinaigrette

150ml olive oil

2 golden shallots, peeled and finely chopped

1 teaspoon Sharwoods mild curry paste

50ml lemon juice

1 portion parsnip mash, (recipe page 73)

parsnip crisps

1 parsnip, peeled

vegetable oil for frying

30 medium-size scallops, roe off

30 long slices pancetta

3 tablespoons light olive oil

juice of ½ lemon

salad leaves to serve

1 small bunch chives, finely chopped

Serves 6

To make the vinaigrette, heat 1 tablespoon of the olive oil in a small pan. Gently sweat the shallots until soft, then stir through the curry paste. In a food processor or upright blender, purée shallots until smooth. Transfer to a bowl and whisk in the lemon juice, followed by the remaining olive oil. Set aside until required.

Prepare the parsnip mash and set aside until required.

To make the parsnip crisps, heat the oil in a shallow frypan to high heat. Using a potato peeler, slice the parsnip into long, thin strips. Fry until golden, drain on absorbent paper then store in an airtight container until required.

To prepare the scallops, lay the strips of pancetta on a board. Place the outer edge of each scallop at one end of a strip and roll up until the pancetta forms a double layer around the scallop.

Heat a little olive oil in a large, non-stick pan over high heat. Fry the scallops, pancetta-side down, turning several times to crisp all the pancetta. Finish with the face of the scallop on the pan, being careful not to overcook them. Add a squeeze of lemon juice to finish.

Meanwhile, reheat the parsnip purée. Dress a few salad leaves with the curry vinaigrette.

To serve, place a spoonful of parsnip purée in the centre of each plate, then arrange five scallops around it. Place a handful of parsnip crisps on top of the purée, then top with some dressed salad leaves. Drizzle the scallops with a little vinaigrette and scatter with chives.

philip jOhnson

123

roast quail

carrot and cumin salad with coriander and mint dressing

coriander and mint dressing

250ml (1 cup) natural yoghurt

2 golden shallots, peeled and quartered

juice of 1 lemon

pinch of ground, roasted cumin seeds

pinch of dried chilli flakes

2 cups mint leaves, picked and washed

2 cups coriander leaves, picked and washed

sea salt and freshly milled black pepper

carrot and cumin salad

100ml olive oil

4 teaspoons cumin seeds

4 teaspoons black mustard seeds

3 large carrots, peeled and grated

zest of 1 orange

1 tablespoon white wine vinegar

sea salt and freshly milled black pepper

½ cup coriander leaves, picked and washed

6 quail, deboned and butterflied

olive oil for cooking

salt and freshly milled black pepper

Serves 6

To make the coriander and mint dressing, place the yoghurt in a fine sieve over an empty bowl for at least 1 hour to remove the excess water.

Blend the shallots and lemon juice in a food processor to a smooth paste. Add the cumin, chilli flakes, mint and coriander, and season to taste. Blend until smooth. Transfer mixture to a bowl, stir in yoghurt and adjust seasoning.

To make the carrot and cumin salad, heat the olive oil, cumin and mustard seeds in a large saucepan over moderate heat. When the seeds begin to pop, add the grated carrot and orange zest. Cook for a few minutes, stirring well, until the carrot just begins to soften. Add the vinegar and season. Set aside to cool.

To cook the quail, heat a large, heavy-based pan over high heat. Brush quail with olive oil and season. Place quail skin-side down in the hot pan and cook for 2 to 3 minutes, until the skin is crisp and a golden colour. Turn and cook for a further 2 minutes. Remove from pan and rest briefly.

To serve, toss the coriander leaves through the salad then divide among serving plates. Spoon the coriander dressing around the salad, then rest quail on top. Finish with a drizzle of good quality olive oil.

philip johnson

iced cOcOnut terrine

with pineapple and lime salsa

coconut terrine

140g sugar

500ml (2 cups) coconut milk

50g glucose

juice of 3 limes

zest of 1 lime

pineapple sorbet

200g sugar

50g glucose

juice of 1 lemon

800ml pineapple juice

sesame wafers

40ml orange juice

80g castor sugar

40g plain flour

¼ teaspoon ground ginger

40g sesame seeds

40g unsalted butter, melted

15g glacé ginger

pineapple and lime salsa

½ pineapple, preferably gold, finely diced

juice of 1 lime

zest of ½ lime

1 kaffir lime leaf, stem removed, cut into very fine strips

1 teaspoon diced fresh red chilli

few mint leaves, finely sliced

coconut cream to serve

shaved fresh coconut to serve

Serves 6-8

To make the coconut terrine, line a terrine or loaf tin with cling film, leaving an overhang.

In a heavy-based saucepan, dissolve sugar in 100ml coconut milk. Add glucose, lime juice and remaining coconut milk. Bring to the boil.

Cool, then churn in ice-cream machine. Once churned, fold zest through.

Spoon mixture into terrine; smoothing the top with the back of a metal spoon. Cover top with overhang, then wrap the whole terrine or loaf tin in cling film. Freeze overnight or until set.

To make the pineapple sorbet, place sugar, glucose and lemon juice in a heavy-based saucepan with 100ml of the pineapple juice. Bring to boil, reduce heat and simmer until mixture becomes a syrup. Cool, then add remaining pineapple juice. Churn in ice-cream machine.

Preheat oven to 170°C.

To make sesame wafers, line baking sheets with silpat mats or baking paper. In a bowl, combine orange juice and sugar, stirring to dissolve the sugar. Set aside. Sift the flour and ground ginger into a mixing bowl and add the sesame seeds. Stir in the melted butter and orange juice and sugar mixture, incorporating well. Add the glacé ginger.

Spread thin circles of mixture 8cm in diameter onto the baking sheets. Bake for 7 to 10 minutes until golden in colour.

Slide the sheet of baking paper onto a cooling rack to cool wafers completely before removing. Store sesame wafers in an airtight container until required.

To make the pineapple and lime salsa, combine all ingredients in a bowl. Set aside for 15 minutes for flavours to infuse.

To serve, run the base of the terrine or loaf tin briefly under warm water, then carefully tap the terrine out onto a flat tray. Place back in freezer for 1 hour.

Place a spoonful of salsa in the middle of each plate. Slice terrine thickly and place a slice over each serving of salsa. Drizzle coconut cream over and around. Lay a sesame wafer over terrine and top with a scoop of pineapple sorbet and shaved coconut.

philip johnson

stephanie alexander

brisbone

Stephanie, a prolific author of cookbooks, visited Soul to launch the second edition of her famous *The Cook's Companion*. Stephanie's recipes have inspired me over many years and I have used and still continue to use some of them as a source of reference for Soul's menus. They are easy to use and always work.

For Stephanie's book launch, we chose an informal barbecue on the terrace, enabling Stephanie to mix and mingle with the guests. The food comprised our best local produce, the quality of which Stephanie freely endorses and promotes (although she remains, like me, scathing of the presentation of flat-shelled oysters in plastic pottles rather than in their natural shell). Her second edition of *The Cook's Companion* now includes recipes made with traditional New Zealand products.

Stephanie's writing and teaching continues to showcase her as an outspoken champion of good food, quality and diversity.

Stephanie has chosen three recipes for inclusion in this book, a delightful lamb dish and two delicious desserts.

chargrilled lamb racks with panzanella salad

marinade for lamb

½ cup Dijon mustard

2 tablespoons light soya sauce

2 tablespoons plain flour

2 tablespoons olive oil

2 teaspoons finely chopped fresh rosemary leaves

freshly milled black pepper

4 racks of lamb
(16 portions)

panzanella salad

300g sourdough bread, at least 1 day old

8 ripe tomatoes, cubed

2 small red onions, peeled and minced

1 telegraph cucumber, diced

2 sticks celery, finely sliced

3 cloves garlic, peeled and crushed

¾ cup fresh basil leaves, torn into small pieces

½ cup extra virgin olive oil

3 tablespoons red wine vinegar

sea salt and freshly milled black pepper

Serves 6

Mix all marinade ingredients together and smear liberally over meat. (The soya sauce can be substituted for a hot pepper relish or puréed chutney.) Leave for 1 hour.

To make the panzanella, remove crust and cut or tear bread into small pieces. Place in a bowl and sprinkle with cold water until the bread is moist but not soggy. Add vegetables, garlic and basil. Dress with oil and vinegar, toss well and adjust seasoning. Allow to stand for 30 minutes so the flavours blend.

Cook the lamb racks for 10 minutes on each side on the grill of a barbecue. If you have a cover on your barbecue, cover the meat for the last 10 minutes. Allow the surface of the meat to sear and seal well before attempting to turn. The paste will cook to a dark crust.

Let the rack rest for 5 minutes. Separate the cutlets and serve alongside the panzanella salad.

stephanie alexander

Oeufs à la neige

floating islands

praline

250g nuts (peanut, almond or cashew), blanched or skinned, and toasted

sweet almond oil or other neutral-flavoured oil

1 cup sugar

½ cup water

egg custard

1 cup milk

1 cup cream

1 vanilla pod, split

5 egg yolks

½ cup castor sugar

meringue

2 litres water

1 vanilla pod

5 egg whites

pinch of salt

60g castor sugar

Serves 6

To make the praline, spread nuts over a lightly oiled baking sheet. Over high heat, dissolve sugar in water and cook until a deep amber. Pour over nuts and let harden.

Break into pieces and store in a screw-top jar. A finer praline is obtained by processing small pieces in a food processor (a terrible noise!) or wrapping the pieces in a clean tea towel and crushing them with a meat mallet.

To make the custard, in a heavy-based saucepan bring milk, cream and vanilla pod to simmering. In a bowl, whisk egg yolks with sugar until light and foamy, then whisk in warm milk and cream. Return to a clean pan and cook over a moderate heat for at least 10 minutes, stirring constantly with a wooden spoon, until mixture thickens and coats back of spoon. (If you have a thermometer, 82–85°C is the ideal temperature for a properly thickened custard.) Strain into a cold bowl, then scrape in some vanilla seeds from the split pod. Allow to cool.

To make the meringue, in a wide saucepan bring water and vanilla pod to simmering. Hold water at a bare simmer. Whisk egg whites with salt until soft peaks form. Sprinkle castor sugar over and continue to whisk until firm and shiny.

Dip a serving spoon into the hot water, then use it to scoop a ball of meringue mixture into the barely simmering water. Scoop out five more balls, wiping the spoon clean each time. Poach gently for 5 minutes, turning with a slotted spoon after 2½ minutes.

Remove cooked meringues with a slotted spoon and leave to cool on a clean, folded tea towel.

No more than 30 minutes before serving, swirl a little raspberry sauce (recipe page 84 - optional) through the custard and drizzle a small amount of honey caramel sauce (recipe page 108) over the meringues.

To serve, pour cold custard into a large serving platter or individual bowls and float meringues on top. Scatter crushed praline over.

fresh strawberry tart

When Stephanie launched *The Cook's Companion* at Soul, we held an informal barbecue and presented this dessert as individual tarts with mixed strawberries and raspberries.

pastry cream
2 cups milk
1 vanilla pod, split
6 egg yolks
¾ cup castor sugar
50g cornflour

1 portion shortcrust pastry
  (recipe page 136)

250g strawberries
100g raspberries (optional)
¼ cup redcurrant or
  blackcurrant jelly, warmed

icing sugar for dusting

To make the pastry cream, in a saucepan scald milk with vanilla pod. In a bowl, beat egg yolks with sugar and cornflour until thick. Pour in milk and whisk until smooth.

Return mixture to a clean saucepan and stir continuously over a moderate heat until pastry cream is smooth, thickened and has come to a boil. Beat vigorously for 1 minute.

Pour through a coarse strainer resting over a bowl. Wash and dry vanilla pod and reserve for another use.

Press cling film onto pastry cream to prevent a skin forming, and cool.

To make the tart, roll out pastry to 3mm thick and line an 18cm-diameter, loose-bottomed flan tin. Trim edges and chill for 1 hour.

Heat oven to 200°C. Blind bake pastry for 20 minutes. Remove weights and tinfoil and allow to cool.

Spread pastry cream over pastry case. Arrange strawberries (and raspberries, if using) thickly over cream, either in tightly fitting concentric circles or piled on for a more random effect. With a large spoon, glaze tart with melted jelly. Dust with icing sugar.

Eat within an hour or two, before the pastry cream softens the base of the tart.

basics

Basic vinaigrette

This recipe is best made the night before use to allow the flavours to infuse. It will keep for a month in the fridge.

100ml white wine vinegar
35g Dijon mustard
½ teaspoon Worcestershire sauce
1 cup olive oil
1 cup canola oil
1 tablespoon water
salt and freshly milled black pepper
½ clove garlic, peeled

Makes 650ml

Combine vinegar, mustard and Worcestershire sauce in a mixer with a whisk attachment. Whisking on high speed, slowly drizzle in the oils.

Correct the consistency with the water, season to taste and add the garlic clove to infuse. Bottle and store.

Celery salsa verde

I love this salsa verde as an accompaniment to grilled fish, especially salmon, or chicken. It lasts well in the fridge for up to 10 days.

½ cup parsley leaves, roughly chopped and tightly packed
½ cup basil leaves, roughly chopped and tightly packed
125g pickled vegetables
65g capers
4 stalks celery (approximately 200g), peeled
1 whole green pepper (capsicum), deseeded and roughly chopped
75g anchovies
1 clove garlic, peeled and finely chopped
½ cup roughly chopped white bread (preferably ciabatta), crusts removed

sea salt and freshly milled black pepper
½ cup olive oil

Makes 650ml

In a food processor, place the parsley and basil. Blend for approximately 2 minutes. Slowly add next nine ingredients. Keep blending until smooth, slowly adding oil as you would when making mayonnaise. This sauce should be the consistency of a thick mayonnaise. You may have to blend half the mixture at a time to achieve this. All the flavours should blend harmoniously, with a predominant flavour of celery, anchovy and basil, and the acidity of the capers and pickled vegetables.

Fish non glacé

This is a base fish sauce, to which other flavours can be added.

50g unsalted butter
1 cup shallots, peeled and finely chopped
¼ cup fennel bulb, peeled and finely chopped
500ml Noilly Prat dry vermouth
750ml fish stock (recipe page 138)
750ml cream
2 sprigs tarragon
2 sprigs chervil
1 sprig thyme
1 sprig flat-leaf parsley

Makes 1200mls

In a saucepan, melt the butter, add the shallots and fennel, and cook until soft but not coloured. Moisten with the Noilly Prat and continue cooking until the liquid is reduced by three-quarters.

Add fish stock, bring back to the simmer and reduce by half.

Add cream and herbs and bring back to the simmer for 10 minutes.

Remove from the heat and pass through a wet, muslin-lined chinois or fine strainer.

Mayonnaise

2 egg yolks

2 teaspoons Dijon mustard

salt and freshly milled black pepper

225ml canola or soya oil

125ml olive oil (not extra virgin)

2 teaspoons lemon juice or white wine vinegar

Makes 400ml

Combine the yolks, mustard, salt and pepper in a blender or mixer and whisk until smooth. Slowly drizzle in the oils, a little at a time, while continuing to whisk on high speed.

Add white wine vinegar or lemon juice. Adjust seasoning.

If the mayonnaise curdles, it can be saved by taking another egg yolk and slowly adding the failed mayonnaise to it, while continually whisking.

For lemon mayonnaise, add the zest and juice of 6 lemons.

If using this recipe to make Caesar dressing or tartare sauce, do not add salt and pepper.

nage

Sweetcorn nage

'Nage' simply means 'swimming'. In this case, it is the sweetcorn kernels that are swimming in a subtle, light chicken stock simmered with herbs. This nage is the basis for many of my butter sauces, buttered nages and frothed sauces. It was born of my love for the classic beurre blanc and beurre rouge, tempered with the realisation of a need for restraint!
In this much lighter and less cloying version, the sweetcorn delivers a sweetness and allows the sauces to be simmered — quite the opposite of beurre blanc, which splits easily when heated. The starch molecules wrap themselves around the fat molecules and hold them in suspension.

Peter Thornley introduced this nage to Soul when he was the executive chef. We still use it now.

3 litres chicken stock (recipe page 138)

750g sweetcorn kernels, cut from the cob

1 sprig thyme

Makes 2 litres

In a large saucepan, bring the chicken stock to a simmer. Add the sweetcorn kernels and thyme. Bring the liquid back to a simmer and reduce to 2 litres, skimming constantly.

Pour the nage into a bowl through a wet, muslin-lined chinois and chill by setting over ice.

Refrigerate for 1 to 2 days or freeze in amounts appropriate to your recipes.

Buttered nage

This is the basic recipe to which any manner of ingredients can be added to bring the buttered nage to life.

500ml sweetcorn nage

300g butter, cut into 1cm cubes

sea salt and freshly milled white pepper

2 sprigs thyme

Makes 800ml

Place the sweetcorn nage into a saucepan and bring to a simmer. Slowly whisk butter into the nage.

Season to taste with salt and pepper. Add the thyme 1 minute before straining the buttered nage as this keeps the flavour fresh and alive.

Pass the buttered nage through a muslin-lined chinois or fine strainer into a clean saucepan. Cover with a paper lid and keep warm until required.

Neutral veal and chicken jus

This is a neutral-based jus which is used as the starting point for finished sauces. For example, to make a tarragon sauce for lamb, add browned lamb bones and tarragon to the jus. For chicken, add browned chicken wings. For a red wine sauce, add red wine.

3 tablespoons unsalted butter

½ cup diced shallot

1 large clove garlic, peeled and cut in half

150gm lamb, chicken, rabbit, hare, venison or veal bones (depending upon required finished flavour), roasted and chopped into 2cm pieces

30ml brandy

200ml dry white wine

500ml reduced veal stock (recipe page 140)

300ml chicken stock (recipe page 138)

1 sprig thyme

1 small bay leaf

Makes 400ml approximately

In a saucepan, melt the butter over a moderate to high heat. Reduce the heat and sweat the shallots and garlic. Cook until the shallots are just about to caramelise.

Add the chopped bones to the shallots. Deglaze the pan with brandy, then add the wine and reduce completely.

Cover the bones with the veal and chicken stocks. Add the thyme and bay leaf. Simmer for 20 to 25 minutes.

Pass the jus through a wet, muslin-lined chinois at least four times, rinsing the muslin between passes. Don't try to push the jus through with a ladle as it will make the jus cloudy.

Return jus to a clean saucepan over a moderate heat, add any herbs if required and infuse for 1 minute. Use as required.

pastry

Short pastry

1¼ cups plain flour

⅔ cup chopped cold unsalted butter

2 tablespoons sugar

¾ teaspoon salt

1 egg yolk

3 tablespoons ice water

Using an electric mixer or by hand, combine the flour, butter, sugar and salt in a large bowl until pebble-sized balls form. Combine the egg yolk and ice water in a small bowl. Add to the flour mixture and mix until the dough starts to stick together.

On a floured benchtop, pat the dough into a disk, and cover with cling film. Chill for at least 1 hour.

Sweet shortcrust pastry

200g plain flour

1 teaspoon salt

1 tablespoon sugar

100g cold unsalted butter, diced

1 egg

2 teaspoons water

Blend the flour, salt, sugar and butter in a food processor until the mixture resembles breadcrumbs. Lightly mix the egg and water and add to processor while the motor is running. As soon as the pastry starts to form a ball, stop mixing, scoop pastry onto a sheet of cling film, wrap and press into a flattish disc. Chill for 1 hour before use.

Polenta

There are two varieties of polenta available. For this recipe, do not buy 'quick cook' polenta or the kind that will cook in five minutes or less. They are better for soft polenta dishes.

750ml chicken stock (recipe page 138)

1 teaspoon salt

125g polenta

50g unsalted butter, cubed

75g parmesan cheese, freshly grated

salt and freshly milled white pepper

Serves 12

In a large saucepan, bring the stock to the boil and add the salt.

Lower the heat to a simmer and slowly add the polenta, stirring with a whisk until completely blended. It will start to bubble and spit.

Reduce to as low a heat as possible. Cook the polenta for 45 minutes, stirring from time to time with a wooden spoon to prevent a skin forming on the top. The polenta is cooked when it falls away from the sides of the pan and has become very dense.

Stir in the butter and parmesan and season to taste.

Pour the polenta into a 20cm x 10cm tray at least 3cm deep, and spread evenly straight away as it will set quickly.

Allow to cool and slice into required portions.

Potato gnocchi

500g Agria potatoes

1 cup plain flour

1 egg, whisked

¼ cup parmesan cheese, freshly grated

½ teaspoon freshly grated nutmeg

1 tsp salt

Serves 4–6

Preheat the oven to 180°C. Bake unpeeled potatoes for 1 hour or until completely cooked. Cut in half, scoop out the flesh and pass it through a mouli or rub through a sieve.

Place the potato flesh in a bowl and make a well in the middle. Add the flour, egg, parmesan, nutmeg and salt. Fold all the

ingredients together gently to form a dough. Do not over-work the dough or the gnocchi will become heavy and tough. Use a little more flour if necessary to make a dough that is smooth and not sticky.

Bring a large saucepan of salted water to the boil. Test the dough by placing a small piece in the water. It is cooked when it floats to the surface. Taste for seasoning and add more salt if necessary.

Shape the dough into a ball and divide into four. On a lightly floured surface, roll out each section into a sausage about 1cm thick. Cut into 3cm slices on the bias. Cook as above in boiling salted water.

Remove the cooked gnocchi from the boiling water with a slotted spoon as they come to the surface, and plunge them into ice water. Drain on absorbent paper for 4 to 5 minutes. Once dry, store on a lightly oiled tray in the refrigerator.

Serve with duck confit (see page 42) or potato gnocchi with ragoût (see page 100).

Risotto base

75ml olive oil

150g butter

1 cup finely diced onion

500g risotto rice (Carnaroli)

1 fresh bay leaf

100ml dry white wine

2 litres white chicken stock, boiling (recipe page 138)

Serves 6

In a saucepan over a medium to high heat, heat the oil and butter. Add the onion and sauté until transparent and without colour. Add the rice and sauté without colouring for a further 1 to 2 minutes.

Add the bay leaf and wine. Stir until the wine has been absorbed. Continue stirring and slowly add the stock, a little at a time. Add more stock only when the previous amount has been absorbed. (Adding stock one-third at a time is quite acceptable.)

Cook until the rice is almost cooked through, stirring continuously, until almost all liquid is reduced. Cool the rice as quickly as possible to prevent further cooking. To cool quickly, turn the rice out onto a tray and spread it thinly, or put into the refrigerator. This risotto base will keep for up to 2 days, refrigerated in a covered container

Stocks

Chicken stock

A light and subtle, almost neutral-flavoured stock for use in risottos, braised white-meat dishes such as rabbit and veal, and in soups. It is also the base for the sweetcorn nage.

1kg chicken frames, cut into 3 portions to fit into saucepan
200g chicken wings
100g chicken feet (optional)
6 litres water
1 cup diced leek, white part only (2cm dice)
½ cup diced onion (2cm dice)
1 tablespoon diced celery (2cm dice)
½ clove garlic
1 bouquet garni consisting of:
   2 sprigs flat-leaf parsley
   2 sprigs thyme
   1 bay leaf

Makes 3 litres

Wash the chicken frames under cold running water to remove any blood and organs. Trim and discard any fat.

In a large stockpot, bring 3 litres of water to the boil. Add the chicken frames, wings and feet. Simmer for 1 to 2 minutes.

Drain the chicken in a colander and rinse under cold running water. Clean the stockpot.

Place the chicken back into the cleaned stockpot and cover with 3 litres of cold water. Bring to the boil, reduce heat to a simmer and skim.

Add the vegetables, garlic and bouquet garni and simmer for 1 hour, skimming regularly. (In order to achieve a totally clear stock, regular skimming is essential.)

Remove from heat and stand for 10 minutes so any remaining debris falls to the bottom of the stockpot. Pass stock through a wet, muslin-lined chinois or a fine strainer. Do not force the stock through or it will be cloudy.

Cool as quickly as possible by placing the container in iced water, stirring the stock occasionally.

Keep for 1 to 2 days in the refrigerator or freeze in convenient amounts if not required immediately.

Fish stock

When selecting the fish bones and heads for this recipe, use those from large-boned, deep-sea fish such as large snapper, blue-nose, hapuku or tuna. Avoid oily fish such as the mackerel family or rock cod, which make the stock cloudy. Have your fishmonger remove the eyes, gills and intestines, and cut the fish bones into 5cm square pieces.
Bill Marchetti

2kg fish bones
100ml olive oil
200g butter
500g diced onion, carrot, celery and leek (total)
350ml white wine
2 bay leaves
½ bunch parsley stalks
10 peppercorns
1 cup fresh fennel sprigs (in season)

In a large bowl, soak the fish bones with cold running water for at least 2 hours. Remove all the blood clots and fat pieces.

In a large, heavy-bottomed, stainless-steel stockpot, heat the oil and butter without browning the butter. (This may seem a large amount of butter, but it helps to give the stock a lovely yellow colour and brings more flavour out of the bones.)

Add the diced vegetables and sauté for about 15 minutes or until they are tender. Add the fish bones and sauté until all the bones have whitened, but avoid browning them.

Add the white wine and over a very high heat evaporate some of the alcohol. (This should take no more than 10 minutes.) Add the bay leaves, parsley stalks, peppercorns and fennel sprigs.

Just cover the bones with cold water. Bring the stock to a boil, turn down the heat to a simmer and skim constantly. After 35 minutes, take the stock off the heat, set aside and let it infuse for another 35 minutes.

Strain the stock through muslin or a very fine strainer. Use a ladle to transfer the stock from the pot to the strainer. Take great care not to break up the bones, as this will make the stock cloudy. Let it rest and cool for 1 hour, then remove the excess fat floating on top and decant.

Golden chicken stock

A light golden stock, made from gently browned bones. It can be used either as a stand-alone stock or sauce base, or blended with veal stock to lighten sauces and give further structure and layering of flavour and complexity.

1kg chicken frames, cut into 3 portions to fit into saucepan
200g chicken wings
100g chicken feet (optional)
3 litres water
½ cup each, 2cm diced onion, carrot, leek (white part only)
2 tablespoons diced celery (2cm dice)
¼ cup tomato, coarsely chopped
½ clove garlic
1 bouquet garni consisting of:
   2 sprigs flat-leaf parsley
   2 sprigs thyme
   1 bay leaf

Makes 3 litres

Preheat your oven to 210°C.

Wash the chicken under cold running water to remove any blood and organs. Trim and discard any fat.

Place the chicken in a single layer on a wire rack set over a roasting dish. Roast until golden (approximately 30 minutes). Reserve the fat for confit or for roasting potatoes.

Place the chicken in a colander and rinse under cold running water to remove any remaining fat.

Place the chicken into a stockpot and cover with cold water. Bring to the boil, reduce heat and simmer. Skim constantly.

Once the liquid is at a consistent simmer add the vegetables, garlic and bouquet garni. Bring slowly back to the simmer, and simmer for 3 hours. Keep skimming to achieve a clear golden stock.

Remove from heat and stand for 10 minutes, so any remaining debris falls to the bottom of the stockpot. Pass stock through a wet-muslin-lined chinois or fine strainer. Do not force the stock through or it will become cloudy.

Cool as quickly as possible by placing the container in iced water and stirring the stock occasionally.

Keep for 1 to 2 days in the refrigerator or freeze if not required immediately.

To reduce the stock:

Place the stock in a large saucepan and bring slowly to the simmer. Simmer until the stock reduces by approximately one-third. The reduced stock should have a bright golden colour and a sauce-like consistency.

Pass through a wet-muslin-lined chinois or fine strainer. Wetting the muslin will help the reduced stock pass through easily.

Keep in the refrigerator in a covered container, or freeze if not required immediately.

Meat stock (brodi di carne)

I prefer to use both beef and chicken in my stock for a fuller, richer flavour. The sinews in shin beef give it a solid gelatinous texture. Buy beef like osso buco, sliced with the bone into thick slices. For a lighter stock, use chicken only.
As with all stock, the ratio of meat to water is crucial here. There should be just enough water for all the ingredients to 'swim'. The cooking time should not be longer than 6 hours, as a duller flavour will result from excess cooking.

                             Bill Marchetti

1kg shin beef
1 boiling fowl (approximately 1kg)
500g beef bones
500g diced celery, carrot and onion (total)
1 bouquet garni, consisting of:
   4 bay leaves
   handful parsley stalks
   20 peppercorns
   3 cloves garlic
   sprigs of fresh thyme, oregano and basil
pinch rock salt

Makes approximately 3 litres

Place all ingredients in a large stockpot. Just cover with cold water and bring to the boil. Turn down to a simmer and cook for about 6 hours. Skim the pot constantly.

Strain the stock, first through a chinois, then through muslin.

Let it settle and cool for 1 hour, then decant it, discarding all the sediment. Divide into suitable-size containers and freeze.

Mushroom stock

¼ cup chopped Spanish onions

2 cloves garlic, peeled

700g assorted mushrooms (e.g. shiitake, Portobello, button)

3 cups water

Makes 1½ cups

Place all ingredients in a medium-size saucepan. Simmer over medium heat for 40 minutes, then strain through a fine-mesh sieve. Return liquid to the saucepan and continue to simmer for 20 minutes, or until you have about one and a half cups of stock.

Veal stock

3 veal shin or knuckle bones (approximately 1.5kg)

½ pig's trotter, split lengthways

1 red onion, peeled and halved

2 medium carrots, peeled

4 celery stalks

2 garlic cloves, peeled

1 cup fresh diced tomatoes

a few flat-leaf parsley stalks

5 black peppercorns

3 bay leaves or thyme sprigs

sea salt

Preheat the oven to 180°C. Place the veal bones in a large roasting dish and brown gently for 40 minutes. Remove from oven and deglaze the pan with a little boiling water, scraping up any caramelised juices from the bottom.

While the bones are roasting, place the pig's trotter in a saucepan with enough cold water to cover, bring slowly to a simmer for 1 to 2 minutes. Remove from saucepan and rinse under cold water.

Put the bones and the pig's trotter, the roasting juices and all the other ingredients except the salt and the tomatoes into a large pan, cover with 3 litres of cold water, and bring to the boil, skimming off the scum as it comes to the surface. Lower the heat and simmer gently for 2 hours.

Add the fresh diced tomatoes and simmer gently for another 20 minutes. Strain, season with salt, and leave to cool. If not using immediately, keep in a refrigerator for up to two days.

To reduce the stock:

Put the stock in a clean saucepan (approximately 3 litres). Bring stock slowly to a simmer and simmer until the stock reduces to about 1 litre. The stock should be a golden-brown colour and a sauce-like consistency. Pass through a muslin-lined chinois. Store in a refrigerator or freeze until required.

Vegetable stock

A light, aromatic stock; this can be frothed or lifted to new heights with cinnamon, vanilla, thyme, lemon grass and basil. Vegetable stock deteriorates quickly, but it can be refrigerated for 1 to 2 days or frozen.

½ lemon, cut into wedges

1½ cups diced onion (0.5cm dice)

½ cup diced leeks (0.5cm dice)

½ cup diced celery (0.5cm dice)

1½ cups diced carrot (0.5cm dice)

¾ cup fennel bulb (0.5cm dice)

30g garlic

5 white peppercorns

5 pink peppercorns

1 bay leaf

2 star anise

3 litres water

200ml dry white wine

2 sprigs tarragon

2 sprigs basil

6 coriander seeds, crushed

4 sprigs chervil

4 sprigs flat-leaf parsley

Makes 3 litres

Place the first 11 ingredients into a stockpot. Add the water and wine and bring to the simmer. Simmer for 20 minutes.

Add the herbs, pushing them down into the liquid. Remove from heat.

When cool, pour into containers and cover. Sit for 24 hours in the fridge to allow herbs to infuse.

Pass through wet muslin or a fine strainer, and discard vegetables and herbs.

glossary

Ingredients

Most of the following ingredients can be found in good supermarkets, food stores such as Sabato or Zarbo, or Asian emporiums like Wah Lee or Tai Ping.

amaretti biscuits — Italian, almond-flavoured cookies.

burghul (or bulgur) — cracked wheat that has been steamed, dried and crushed.

cabernet sauvignon vinegar — vinegar made from cabernet sauvignon grapes. Plain red wine vinegar can be substituted.

candlenut — a type of nut from Malaysia, with a similar taste and texture to macadamia nuts.

champagne vinegar — white wine vinegar made from champagne.

Chèvre de Bellay goat's cheese — a fresh French goat's cheese. New Zealand goat camembert can be substituted.

ciabatta — 'slipper bread', an Italian crusty white loaf. Now widely available in supermarkets and bakeries.

clear thyme honey — clear honey infused with thyme. If not available use any clear runny honey.

ebly — par-cooked wheat grain from whole, pre-cooked durum wheat grains.

Ferron superfino carnaroli rice — the finest Italian rice, perfect for risotto. Other risotto rices can also be used.

fig vincotta — a grape syrup made from aged wine vinegar infused with figs.

galangal powder — an Asian spice from the ginger family, available from Asian food stores.

Gaeta green olives — large green olives from Sicily.

gozo dumpling wrappers — Japanese wheat-cake wrappers.

Gusto apple syrup — a concentrated apple syrup.

jou jou bread — Lebanese flat bread.

Maldon sea salt — flaky sea salt from Maldon in England.

mirin — sweetened sake (Japanese rice wine).

Mount Hector cheese — goat's-style camembert from Kapiti Cheese Co.

mountain bread — thin, unleavened bread.

Ortiz anchovies — artisan Spanish anchovies.

pancetta — Italian-style bacon.

pomegranate molasses — a tangy and tart syrup from the Middle East, made from cooked-down pomegranate juice.

Puhoi goat's feta — a local cheese, made north of Auckland.

sake — Japanese rice wine.

scampi — a large, prawn-like crustacean, also known as langoustine or baby deep-sea lobster.

skordalia — a Greek garlic sauce.

Strega — Italian liqueur. Can be substituted with Galliano.

tamari — wheat-free soya sauce.

Methods & equipment

blind bake — to cook pastry without allowing it to rise. Tinfoil or baking paper is placed over the pastry case, then weights or baking beans are used to weigh it down while it is cooked. Filling is added after cooking.

baking parchment — non-stick baking paper.

cartouche — a paper lid used to prevent a skin forming on a liquid, or in place of a saucepan lid.

chinois — 'Chinese cap', a conical-shaped strainer.

deglaze — to add a liquid, usually wine, to a pan to release sediment.

double boiler — two pots designed to fit together, with a single lid. The larger pot holds hot water and provides a gentle, even heat to the top pan.

galette pan — small ovenproof frypan (approximately 10cm in diameter).

jelly bag — a bag used for straining liquids.

julienned — cut into thin strips.

making a bouquet garni — wrap 3 sprigs of thyme, 3 bayleaves and 12 whole peppercorns in cheesecloth and tie with string.

mirepoix — a mixture of roughly chopped carrot, celery and onion used in stock-making.

refresh in iced water — also blanch. To dip vegetables briefly into iced water, to prevent loss of colour.

scald (milk) — bring nearly to the boil, stirring continually, to prevent a protein skin forming on the surface.

silpat mats — reusable non-stick mats used for baking.

egg sabayon —eggs whisked to the point where the fluid falls from the beater in a thick stream that folds on itself and then dissolves.

whiz stick — hand-held beater.

index

soul bar & bistro